Show Don't Tell

How to Write Stories That Are Vivid, Alive and Engaging

Richard Lowe

The Writing King

The Working Writer's Library Series

Show Don't Tell

Table of Contents

See books by Richard Lowe at

https://masterofworlds.com

Get free publishing insights and industry updates at

https://thewritingking.substack.com

For ghostwriting and book coaching services see

https://thewritingking.com

What's The Difference?

---

*"Don't tell me the moon is shining; show me the glint of light on broken glass."–**Anton Chekhov***

Have you ever read a fiction book or story and thought it seemed lifeless or uninteresting?

Do you wonder why some fiction books that you've written never seem to gain an audience?

The problem is likely that you're telling instead of showing.

Telling pushes your readers away. Showing pulls your readers into your story.

Showing lets readers vividly imagine the elements of your story. Telling does the imagining for them.

Books that show instead of tell hold readers in the story. Books that tell push readers out of it. The difference shows up in reviews, in word of mouth, and in whether readers come back for more.

If you've attended any writing classes, or taken writing in school, you've almost certainly been told that you should show and not tell. Writing teachers pound this into their students. Books repeat it over and over again, beating it into our brains. Writing critique groups harp on the point ceaselessly. Show, don't tell.

"Don't tell that your characters are angry; show the anger."

"Don't tell the fire was hot; show them the heat."

"Don't tell us she walked through the door; show us."

One thing that I used to dislike the most was when somebody told me, “Show, don’t tell.” It didn’t mean anything to me. I just ignored the advice, because it was just a few meaningless words.

Writers in writing critique groups are especially fond of repeating the litany over and over. “You’re telling too much,” was something that I heard constantly, but without any explanation of what it meant.

It seemed to me that it’s a lot easier to say, “Sally felt angry,” than it is to try and describe her in such a way that the reader understands she’s angry. Doesn’t that take a lot more words?

What does it really mean to say, “show, don’t tell?”

Let's look at concrete examples to make this clear:

> *TELLING: "Mark was nervous about the job interview."*
>
> *SHOWING: "Mark's palms left damp prints on his resume as he shuffled the papers for the third time. The receptionist's smile felt like a spotlight, and he found himself checking his tie knot again."*
>
> *TELLING: "The house was old and creepy."*
>
> *SHOWING: "Paint peeled from the shutters like dried scabs. The porch sagged under the weight of rotting boards, and somewhere inside, a door creaked on rusty hinges with each gust of wind."*
>
> *TELLING: "Sarah was exhausted after work."*
>
> *SHOWING: "Sarah kicked off her heels and let them clatter across the hardwood. She collapsed onto the couch without bothering to remove her jacket, her purse sliding off her shoulder to the floor."*

In each case, the first version reports information. The second version gives evidence and lets you draw the conclusion.

Telling is giving the reader your own evaluations, conclusions and interpretations of what’s happening in your story, with your characters, or in the background.

Showing means to provide details to your readers so that they can draw conclusions for themselves.

When you tell your readers something, it's as if you're reporting on the situation. Telling adds a level of abstraction–you, the writer–between the reader and the story.

Why is that bad?

When you're writing fiction, the whole idea is to pull your reader into the world that you have created. You want them to see the room, smell the fire, feel the curtains, experience the weight, and understand the pain and suffering. The more you can put your readers into the scene, the more likely they are to keep reading — and to come back for more.

Let's say you see some kittens in a cage at the pet store. You don't want to just look at the kittens through a pane of glass, right? You want to hold them, pet them, and experience them before you decide which one to bring home with you.

Think about buying a car. Most people won't make a purchase based on a photo and some description on the website. They want to go into the dealership, take a test drive, open the windows, hear the engine roaring, and experience how it feels on the freeway.

In both those instances, a report from someone else isn't enough for you to make a purchase. You feel like you must experience the kitten or the car before laying your money down.

Showing is about immersing your reader in the experience of your story.

How do you catch yourself telling instead of showing? Watch for these red flags in your writing:

Watch for emotion words like angry, sad, confused, excited, frustrated, and happy. Look for state-of-being verbs: was, felt, seemed, appeared, looked. Be suspicious of summary statements such as "It had been a long day," "The room was messy," or "He was a difficult person." Watch for conclusion words: obviously, clearly, unfortunately, naturally. And notice character trait announcements: “She was stubborn,” “He was generous,” “They were in love.”

When you find these phrases, stop and ask: "What would my character see, hear, feel, smell, taste, or do that would make the reader reach this same conclusion?"

Here's a simple conversion process:

Identify the telling statement, then ask: “What evidence would prove this?” Replace the statement with concrete, sensory details, and let the reader connect the dots.

Example:

> *TELLING: "The restaurant was busy."*
>
> *EVIDENCE: What proves a restaurant is busy?*
>
> *SHOWING: "The hostess juggled three phone calls while a line of customers snaked past the bar. Servers weaved between tables with loaded trays, and the kitchen doors swung open every few seconds, releasing bursts of sizzling sounds and garlic-scented steam."*

This point is one of the most difficult for new authors to master. Most teachers expect students to pick up the technique after a brief mention, as if it were self-evident. Few graduate understanding how to actually do it.

The purpose of this book is to address that shortcoming and teach you how to effectively show your audience what's happening in your story. Master this technique and the work starts taking care of itself.

Before you read further, you may want to flip to Appendix B at the back of this book. It shows five complete scenes — literary fiction, thriller, romance, science fiction, and young adult — each in three stages: a first draft with telling problems marked, comments explaining every mark, and the revised version after changes. Seeing the before-and-after in your genre will make everything in the chapters that follow more concrete.

Practice: Spot the Difference

Find three sentences in your current draft that begin with a state-of-being verb (was, felt, seemed, looked, appeared). For each one, rewrite it as an action or physical detail. You don't need to make it perfect — just make it concrete.

What is Telling?

"Create a world in front of your readers where they can taste, smell, touch, hear, see, and move. Or else they are likely going to move on to another book." – **Pawan Mishra, On Writing Wonderfully: The Craft of Creative Fiction Writing**

Let's start with telling itself.

What is telling and what is wrong with it?

When you give your reader information in narrative form, you're telling.

Let's look at a few examples.

"It was a hot day." "When they kissed, she could tell that he had been smoking." "She felt relieved." "I ate my food." "The house was unkempt." "She was fat." "Dinner was delicious but smelled bad." "He was terrified." "My stepson was a spoiled brat." "The hotel was romantic." "She was happy." "I was jealous of what Pete got for Christmas." "Dave was uncomfortable." "It was raining outside."

Every one of these is telling. The author is making an evaluation, a conclusion, or an observation about something. Each statement is boring, unimaginative, undramatic, and doesn't pull the reader into the action.

Summaries

Summarizing events is telling — though sometimes, particularly in a prologue, a quick summary is warranted.

However, summarizing everything that's happening is poor writing. Your readers don't want to get a description of what's going on. They want to be part of the scene, to be in the action.

Telling

> *David climbed to the top of the mountain and was tired from the long hike.*

We're told David is tired, but we know nothing else about him — not the effort, the heat, the sensation in his legs.

Showing

> *David gasped, sweating from the exertion of climbing up the steep incline. He'd been walking, and towards the end stumbling, for 2 miles along a cobblestone path that wound its way through sycamore trees and thick shrubbery, and he finally made it to the top. He bent over, breathing hard, his shirt plastered to his chest from the sweat, his breath ragged and his throat parched.*

When telling, the author states facts. David climbed the mountain. He was tired. It's flat. Nothing makes the reader feel anything.

Compare that to the showing version of the same idea. We have the same facts: David climbed to the top of the mountain, and he was tired after a long hike. But we have a much more visual picture of what's happening. He had been walking and stumbled. The path was 2 miles long and it wound past trees and shrubbery. We know it was hot (without being told) because his shirt was plastered to his chest from the sweat, and we know that he went through some exertion and was tired because his breath was ragged, and his throat was parched.

The showing version includes one telling statement — "he made it to the top" — but it earns that compression by how much the surrounding scene shows.

Drawing Conclusions

This is one of the most common telling mistakes: concluding for the reader. This robs the reader of the chance to come to their own conclusions based upon what they see, smell, feel, hear, and can ascertain from the words of the author.

Telling

> *I walked into the room and Lynn looked angry. Did she know?*

That sentence makes a conclusion for the reader. It told the reader that she looked angry. But what does that mean? Was she glaring? Was her face red? Was her fist raised? What was going on here?

Here's the same scene without the telling:

Showing

> *I hesitated, my hand on the doorknob. Taking a deep breath, I turned the knob and pushed the heavy wooden door open slowly. Lynn was sitting at the desk and looked up when she heard a squeak from the hinge of the door. She glared at me, her eyes unwavering and without blinking. A shiver went down my spine. Did she know what I'd done?*

Let's look at one more.

Telling

> *I felt faint from low blood sugar.*

We know the fact. We don't feel it.

Let's try this instead.

Showing

> *My head was spinning, and I stumbled and grabbed hold of the door frame to steady myself. I rubbed my temples, massaging them gently as if trying to squeeze the pain out from my skull. My stomach felt as if hundreds of butterflies were flying around inside. I should have known that skipping breakfast would be a mistake.*

It's longer, but it earns the length.

Notice how the passage doesn't make a conclusion for the reader about what's happening. We don't tell them that the problem is low blood sugar; instead, we show the symptoms and mention that skipping breakfast might be the cause, leaving the diagnosis to the reader.

Vagueness

Using vague language is telling. Your reader should be able to imagine your scene using all their senses. Can you picture it? Can you smell, taste, and hear it? Is it specific enough that you know what's going on, or does their mind need to fill in the gaps?

Telling

> *Jane felt sick.*

What does this mean? What does "sick" mean to the character Jane? Does she have a headache? Is she about to pass out? Or does she have a mild stomachache?

That pulls the reader out of the story — they have to stop and piece together what you mean from the surrounding context.

Showing

> *Jane shivered even though the room was hot. When she stood up, she had to grab the back of the chair. She closed her eyes and swallowed, gasping at the pain within her throat.*

The reader can feel the fever and the sore throat without being told. The specifics do the work.

Adverbs

An adverb is a word that modifies or describes a verb, an adjective, or another adverb. Often, you'll hear them referred to as -ly words. I don't know how many times I've been told by writers and writing critique groups "you're using too many -ly words."

Examples include financially, expertly, wholeheartedly, delightfully, quickly, lightly, eternally, delicately, brutally, sorrowfully, beautifully, truthfully, wickedly, profoundly, and incredibly.

Adverbs typically describe how something was done or the way in which it was done. He was "wholeheartedly involved", "wickedly humorous", or "brutally honest."

Other adverbs tell where an action happened. These include words such as here, there, everywhere, downstairs, outside, and so on. Generally, it's better to be more specific.

Adverbs can also tell when something happened: now, regularly, always.

Adverbs also indicate degree: very, almost, only, rather.

Telling

She was brutally murdered.

One adverb tells us nothing. The second version shows the brutality.

Let's try that again.

Showing

During the autopsy, the pathologist found that she'd been stabbed over 40 times.

The detail of 40 stab wounds does what "brutally" never could — it gives the reader a specific fact and lets them draw their own conclusion.

Telling

He literally went home.

In this case, you can just take the word literally out. It literally (pun intended) has no value. The author intended it to add some emphasis, I guess, to the sentence. Instead, the result is to introduce a momentary doubt in the reader's mind: what does literally mean in this case? Can someone figuratively go home?

Fixed

He drove home.

This isn't a show/tell transformation — it's simply removing a word that adds no meaning. "Literally" belongs in the same category as other redundant adverbs: cut it and the sentence is cleaner and stronger.

Adjectives

An adjective is a word that describes or modifies a noun.

Consider: Jane wore a beautiful dress. I saw a homeless person. What an adorable baby.

Each adjective adds description to the noun. What kind of dress? A beautiful one.

Telling

> *Jane wore a beautiful dress.*

But what does beautiful mean? We can be more specific and add more color to the story.

Showing

> *Jane wore a knee-length, royal blue dress that caught the light when she moved.*

We dropped the vague adjective "beautiful" and replaced it with specific details that let the reader form their own impression. Now we know the dress goes to her knees and is royal blue – and that it catches the light. The reader can decide for themselves whether it's beautiful.

Adjectives aren't necessarily a bad thing in writing. Just examine them to see if you can use more specific terms to better describe something or if the adjective is needed at all.

Linking Verbs

A linking verb is a verb that connects the subject with another word that gives information about the subject.

Jeff was the problem.

The word "was" is the linking verb that connects "Jeff" and "problem" to show the relationship between Jeff and the problem.

The most commonly used linking verbs are: am, is, are, was, were, being, been. There are others as well.

Telling

Jane felt tired.

The linking verb "felt" reports Jane's condition rather than showing it.

Showing

Jane rubbed her eyes and yawned.

Filtering words

These are verbs that describe the character thinking or perceiving something. For example, in the sentence "I realized I'd forgotten my keys" the word "realized" is the filtering word.

Telling

Jim realized he forgot his keys.

How did Jim figure out that he forgot his keys? What problem does it cause?

Showing

Jim reached into his left pocket, frowning when he found there was nothing there. Could his keys be in his right pocket? He checked: no keys. How will he get home now?

That's more dramatic, and considerably more interesting to read.

Practice: Write the Subtext

Find a scene in your current draft where two characters are having a conversation but something unspoken is underneath it. Rewrite 8–12 lines so the real subject is never named – only the surface exchange. If you don't have a draft yet: write two characters discussing what to order for dinner while one of them is trying to end the relationship. Don't let either character name the real subject.

Naming Emotions

Using words such as "disappointed", "upset", or "angry" is telling the reader the emotions of a character. You're evaluating an emotional condition rather than letting your reader see it from context.

Telling

Dave could see that Jim was hurt.

When I read a sentence like that, my thought is "what does that mean?" How does Dave know that Jim was hurt? And what does hurt mean anyway? Is Jim bleeding? Or is he crying because someone hurt his feelings?

Showing

Dave couldn't quite make out what Sally said to Jim, but it must've been something awful because he fell to his knees and started crying.

We can infer the hurt is emotional — no blood is mentioned.

Practice: Convert a Telling Passage

Take a paragraph from your work that contains two or more telling statements. Rewrite the paragraph showing the same information through action, dialogue, or sensory detail. Keep the rewrite under 100 words.

What is Showing?

"The secret of being boring is to say everything." -Voltaire

With telling defined, let's look at what showing actually means — and how to do it.

Vivid imagery is the best way to engage your readers and make them want to immerse themselves in the world of your fiction. This is done not by telling them what's happening, but by showing them.

Showing creates images consisting of multiple senses in your readers' imaginations. Telling, on the other hand, just factually states what's happening whether it be actions, emotions, scenery, or whatever else.

Telling

Dave was hot.

Pretty factual. What you know is that Dave was hot — but the reader might picture a hot day, an attractive man, or someone on a winning streak. The word does too little.

When you're writing a passage that is telling the reader something, you might think you're being unambiguous and factual, but the reader may not agree with you.

Let's look at the same thing written in a sentence that shows Dave being hot.

Showing

> *Rivulets of sweat dripped down Dave's face. His shirt was soaked and clinging to his chest.*

The showing version gives the reader something to picture.

What about the following?

Telling

> *They kissed, and she smelled cigarettes.*

Flat. No feeling, no image.

Showing

> *When her lips touched his, she wrinkled her nose from the earthy stench of tobacco.*

The word "stench" and the wrinkled nose signal disapproval without naming it. Showing the scene injects emotion that telling never could.

Write in Real Time

Write the scenes and action in your story so that they unfold in real time. Don't sum up what happened in the past. It's better that your readers see what's going on moment by moment. This doesn't mean you write in present tense–just tell them what happened in the order that it happened.

A caution here: avoid saying everything that happened. If your character is applying makeup, you don't need to explain each step-by-step action. Just show a few of the steps such as applying the mascara, looking into the mirror, or putting on lipstick.

Don't Give Too Much Detail

No one wants to know every single thing that happens in your story. This applies to dialogue and to descriptions of action.

Think about brushing your teeth. The steps involved are many and quite complex. You must pick up the tube of toothpaste, open it, squeeze the toothpaste onto the brush, and so forth. There is no need to go into all of this in your story. Readers want the scene, not the procedure.

Actions

Don't tell your readers the emotions of your characters, the events that are occurring, or what's going on in the scene.

Show them by using action.

Tell	Show
She was abrasive	Ted was talking, and she interrupted him.
His speech was evasive	He shrugged and looked away, then changed the subject to talk about his mother.
Ted was a coward	As soon as the door opened, Ted dropped his gun and raised his hands.

Break Things Up

One way to show in writing is to break down general things into more specific, smaller parts. Don't just say Jane got out of bed. Instead, show the reader that she opened her eyes, yawned, looked at the clock, cursed because she was late, and jumped onto the floor.

This puts your reader into the scene. Remember, though, too many details slow things down and make the story boring. Find a balance between saying too much and not saying enough.

Be Specific

Use words that are specific to the action, emotion, or event that you're trying to show. General words tend to push readers out of the story because the reader must stop and think to figure out what you're talking about.

Specific words keep readers inside the scene rather than pausing to puzzle out your meaning.

Telling

> *She was happy because she ate a strawberry.*

This tells the reader she's happy — but "happy" is vague.

Let's try it again, focusing on being more specific.

Showing

> *She grinned, her eyes bright, as she reached for the strawberry. "This is my favorite fruit," she said. "I could eat them all day."*

Body language and dialogue together make the happiness concrete without stating it.

Figuratively

You can make your writing shine by using vivid figurative language–similes and metaphors.

A simile compares two things by using the word *like* or *as*. A metaphor also compares two things but does so more directly.

Similes

The purpose of a simile is to make your writing more vivid and powerful. By comparing one thing to another using like or as, a writer plants a specific image in the reader's mind.

She is as innocent as a newborn baby. My headache was so bad it felt like my head was going to explode. She's busy as a bee. He was blind as a bat. In that land, gold was common as dirt. She was tall as a flagpole. He sat there like a bump on a log. My nose was so big it made me stand out like a sore thumb. My throat is dry as a bone.

Note: several of the examples above — busy as a bee, blind as a bat, bump on a log, dry as a bone — are clichés. They are listed here to illustrate the form of a simile, not as models to copy. See the Clichés section below for why you should avoid them.

Metaphors

Metaphors create an effect in a statement. It's boring to say, "time passed quickly." It's more exciting to say, "time is a thief." The reader will get the idea in both cases, but the metaphor creates an impact in the mind of readers. A good metaphor plants an image without requiring explanation.

"Time is a thief" means time passed quickly. "Fade off to sleep" means a person went to sleep. "She was on a roller coaster of emotions" captures the ups and downs. "She reeked of infidelity" makes obvious that a person is cheating. "Jim felt blue" is another way of saying Jim feels sad.

Don't overdo similes and metaphors, because it can make your writing appear to be pretentious or even difficult to read. Also, don't use the first metaphor or simile that comes to mind–because it is probably a cliché.

Clichés

A cliché is an expression that has a general meaning and has been overused over time. They do not bring to mind a specific image or thought. Clichés are neither specific nor vivid — they add nothing to the story.

Clichés tend to annoy readers because they come across as lazy writing or writing without a lot of thought. They make it appear as if the writer lacks originality.

Some examples of clichés include:

Common clichés include "in this day and age," "from the dawn of man," "little did I know," "easy come, easy go," and "every cloud has a silver lining."

Clichés are vague and general in meaning, and sometimes they may not mean anything at all. Because they are not specific and vivid, writers would do well to avoid them. There are exceptions – Piers Anthony built his entire Xanth fantasy series around deliberate, subverted clichés, turning the device into the joke itself.

Thinking

You can show what your character is thinking to reveal emotions. It's natural for people to be thinking in between actions and events, and even between lines of dialogue.

Telling

> *Denise finished reading the book and was happy.*

In the above example, the writer is just telling the reader that Denise had completed reading the book, and then concluded that she was happy about it. Does that mean she likes the book? Or was she happy that it was finally done? Or was she thinking about something else entirely that made her happy?

Showing

> *Denise closed the book and lifted her eyes to stare into the distance. She sighed. That was such a great novel, she thought. I can't wait for the sequel.*

Her thoughts tell us what the bare summary couldn't.

Thoughts are often italicized and tagged, though they don't have to be. The convention depends on how close you want the reader to feel to the character's inner voice.

Choosing the Right Detail

The hardest question in showing is not how to do it — it's which detail to choose. Two writers can both be showing, using nothing but concrete physical detail, and one scene feels alive while the other feels inert. The difference is almost always the detail.

A useful test: does this detail do more than one job? The best showing details carry multiple layers simultaneously — they establish physical reality, reveal character, and carry emotional weight. If a detail only does one of those things, it's working below capacity.

Consider a grieving character sitting in her late mother's kitchen. You could show:

Low-value detail

> *The kitchen was small, with yellow walls and a window above the sink.*

That's accurate and concrete, but it tells us nothing we couldn't infer about any 1970s kitchen. Compare:

High-value detail

> *Her mother had kept the sugar in a tin that said FLOUR on the lid, always. A small private joke that didn't make sense anymore now that there was no one left to be in on it.*

The second detail establishes the kitchen, reveals a relationship (private joke, long habit), and carries the specific quality of this grief — the way minor absurdities become unbearable. It does three jobs.

When choosing a detail, ask: what does this specific person notice in this specific moment? The chef notices the cookware. The grieving daughter notices the mislabeled tin. The right detail is almost never the one that comes to mind first — the first one is usually generic. Push past it to the particular.

Practice: Choose Your Detail

Find a paragraph in your draft that describes a room, object, or location. Identify the details you used. For each one, ask: does this detail do more than one job? If not, replace it with a detail that establishes physical reality and reveals something about the character experiencing it. If you don't have a draft: write three sentences in which a character enters a room they haven't been in for years. Use only physical observation to convey how they feel about being there.

Showing Character Description

Every writer eventually types a sentence like "She was beautiful" or "He had an intimidating presence" and knows it isn't working. The instinct is right. Labels like beautiful, intimidating, kind, or threatening tell the reader what conclusion to draw without giving them the evidence to draw it themselves.

The problem with physical description isn't that writers describe their characters — it's that they describe them the way a police report would. Height, weight, hair color, eye color, notable features. This approach gives the reader a data set, not a person.

The alternative is to show physical appearance through the lens of a perceiving consciousness, and to show personality through behavior, choice, and detail — not adjectives.

Appearance Through a Perceiving Character

When a POV character notices another character's appearance, what they notice and how they describe it reveals both people simultaneously.

Telling

Marcus was tall, with dark hair and an angular face. He had a commanding presence.

Showing

> *He came in while she was mid-sentence and she lost the thread of what she was saying. Not because he was particularly loud, or because he did anything. Her body noticed him before she did — something low and alert, the kind of attention you pay without deciding to. She found the thread again. But she knew where he was in the room for the rest of the evening without looking.*

Nothing here names commanding, intimidating, or predatory. Dana's body responds before she processes it consciously, and she tracks him all evening. The reader draws the conclusion from behavior — both Marcus's and Dana's — not from the author's gloss.

The noticed detail — what a POV character chooses to register — is character revelation. A character who notices another person's shoes is different from a character who notices their hands. A character who notices that someone's smile doesn't reach their eyes is paying a different kind of attention than a character who notices the quality of their clothing.

Telling

Jane was beautiful. She had long dark hair and bright green eyes.

Showing

She wasn't the kind of beautiful you noticed immediately. It arrived in stages — the way she tilted her head when she was listening, the particular quality of her attention, a face that had something going on behind it that made you want to keep looking.

The second version creates a more vivid and memorable impression precisely because it doesn't catalogue features. It describes an experience of noticing.

Personality Through Behavior

The same principle applies to personality. Adjectives like kind, ambitious, cold, generous, or reckless are conclusions. The scene should contain the evidence that lets the reader reach that conclusion.

Telling

Robert was a generous man.

Showing

Robert picked up the check before anyone else reached for it. He did it the way he did everything — without calling attention to the gesture, already talking about something else.

Telling

She was cold and difficult to know.

Showing

She answered every question directly and asked none in return. After twenty minutes of conversation, he realized he had told her his entire history and learned nothing about her except that she preferred her coffee without milk.

The behavior is specific. The reader observes it and draws the same conclusion they would if they witnessed it in real life.

Showing Backstory in a Character's Face and Body

A person's history shows in their physical presence. This is one of the most underused tools for character description — not cataloguing features, but reading what those features imply about a life.

Telling

He'd had a hard life.

Showing

His hands were wrong for his age — roughened and reddened in the way that takes years of outdoor work, not months. The rest of him was careful. Shoes polished. Shirt pressed. The hands gave him away.

Telling

She was a woman who had once been beautiful and knew it.

Showing

She still entered rooms the way beautiful women do — the slight pause at the threshold, the awareness that she was being seen. What had changed was what came after. She didn't wait to see if it was true anymore.

The Danger of the Mirror Scene

One of the most overused devices in fiction is having a character look in a mirror so the author can describe their appearance. It's almost always telling in disguise — the author listing features under the pretense of a character noticing themselves.

If you need readers to know what your protagonist looks like, find a moment when another character notices them, or when the protagonist's physical reality imposes itself on the scene. Let the appearance emerge from action and interaction rather than inventory.

Trust that your readers will build a picture from the details you give them in context. They don't need a complete physical description upfront. They need enough to place the character in the scene, and the rest will accumulate naturally.

Practice: Show Who They Are

Take a character from your draft who is introduced through description. Rewrite the introduction using only what another character notices about them and how the room or scene responds to their presence. No adjectives like handsome, imposing, shy, or confident. If you don't have a draft: write a character arriving at a party described entirely through another character's noticing and the room's response.

Strong Verbs

English gives you hundreds of verbs for any action. You can reach for bland, general ones — or you can find the verb that makes the sentence vivid.

Here are specific examples of weak verbs transformed into strong ones:

MOVEMENT VERBS:

WEAK: "She went to the store quickly."

STRONG: "She raced to the store." / "She darted to the store."

WEAK: "He walked slowly down the hall."

STRONG: "He shuffled down the hall." / "He crept down the hall."

SPEAKING VERBS:

WEAK: "He said loudly."

STRONG: "He bellowed." / "He roared." / "He shouted."

WEAK: "She said quietly."

STRONG: "She whispered." / "She murmured." / "She breathed."

EMOTIONAL VERBS:

WEAK: "She was angry and left."

STRONG: "She stormed out." / "She slammed the door behind her."

WEAK: "He was sad about the news."

STRONG: "He slumped in his chair." / "His shoulders sagged."

Common weak verbs to avoid: went, said, was, looked, seemed, felt, appeared, got, had

Strong alternatives exist for every one of these. Your writing will immediately become more vivid when you eliminate them.

Here's an example of a weak verb.

Sally ran home.

Accurate, but flat.

Here are several alternatives, each producing a different picture:

Sally rushed home.

That's better — it implies she's moving faster than normal. Here are a few more:

Sally jogged home.

Sally raced home.

Sally hustled home.

Sally sprinted home.

Each different verb produces a different picture of the action in your reader's mind.

A stronger verb is always preferable to propping up a weaker one with an adverb.

Sally quickly ran home.

Yes, the adverb "quickly" does tell the reader that she's moving fast, but the following sentence works better.

Sally rushed home.

This doesn't mean that adverbs are always wrong. Sometimes the best way to convey an action in the most specific manner is to modify a verb with an adverb.

Here are some instances where adverbs make sense.

*Donna **utterly** rejected his advances.*

*David **completely** understood the problem.*

*I was so angry I **nearly** quit.*

In each of these cases, the adverb intensifies or amplifies the verb or other word that is being modified.

Still, a stronger verb is usually better than propping up a weak one with an adverb.

*Donna **shunned** his advances.*

*David **mastered** the problem.*

*I was so angry I **almost** quit.*

In the third sentence, "almost" is appropriate because it qualifies the degree of the action.

Another problem is that many adverbs are redundant, and state something that's already been said.

*David screamed **loudly** at the monster that was attacking him.*

In this case, the adverb "loudly" is not necessary and is redundant because it's not possible to scream quietly.

*Donald whispered **quietly**.*

The adverb "quietly" is not necessary in the sentence.

Here are some more examples with the adverbs in bold.

> *The money reverted* ***back*** *to the rightful owner.*
>
> *The donkey bolted* ***quickly*** *out of the barn.*
>
> *Donna tiptoed* ***soundlessly*** *out of the room.*

Each of the bolded adverbs can be removed from the sentence and the meaning will remain the same.

Finding the Right Verb

> *The real work of strong verbs isn't swapping one word for another from a list. It's asking: what exactly is happening, and what is the most precise word for that specific motion, sound, or action?*
>
> *Consider a character leaving a room. The verb "walked" is technically accurate but tells you almost nothing. What kind of walking?*

She walked out of the room.

Now consider the alternatives, each carrying different meaning:

She slipped out of the room. (quiet, perhaps furtive) She trudged out of the room. (heavy, reluctant, exhausted) She swept out of the room. (dramatic, purposeful) She ducked out of the room. (quick, avoiding notice) She stumbled out of the room. (clumsy, distressed) She retreated from the room. (defeated, backing away) She bolted from the room. (sudden, frightened)

Each verb creates a different scene. The same action — person leaves room — becomes seven different characters with seven different emotional states and seven different relationships to what they're leaving.

The verb is doing showing's work. You don't need "she walked out of the room, embarrassed" when "she retreated from the room" already carries the emotion.

Extended Example: Transforming a Passage

Here is a paragraph that uses weak verbs throughout:

Weak Version

He went into the kitchen. She was at the table with papers in front of her. He got a glass from the cabinet and put some water in it. He looked at her but didn't say anything. She moved some papers and then looked at him.

Every verb is as plain and generic as possible. The scene has no texture, no character, no feeling.

Strong Version

He drifted into the kitchen. She sat hunched over the table, papers fanned around her. He pulled a glass from the cabinet and filled it, staring at the faucet. She didn't look up. He turned. She'd gathered the papers into a pile and was pressing them flat with one hand, over and over.

The same scene — man enters, woman is at table with papers, they don't speak — but now it has a quality, a mood, a particular tension. "Drifted" tells us he's uncertain or directionless. "Hunched over" tells us the woman is absorbed or burdened. "Staring at the faucet" tells us he's avoiding looking at her. "Pressing them flat with one hand, over and over" shows her agitation without naming it.

The strong verbs didn't just replace the weak ones — they did work the weak ones couldn't do.

The Practice

When you finish a draft, go through it looking for your default verbs: went, got, was, looked, moved, said, felt, seemed. For each one, ask: what exactly happened? Then find the most specific word for that specific action. Not just "walked" but how she walked. Not just "said" but whether she announced, muttered, confessed, snapped, offered.

You won't find a perfect strong verb for every line. Sometimes "said" is exactly right — it's invisible, which is sometimes what you need. But the habit of looking makes your writing progressively more specific and your scenes progressively more alive.

Practice: Replace the Verb

Take a page from your draft and find every instance of walked, went, said, looked, and moved. For each one, ask: what is the most specific verb for this exact action by this exact character in this exact moment? Replace at least five. If you don't have a draft: write "She left the room" seven different ways, each with a different verb that implies a different emotion. No adverbs allowed.

Telling In Dialog

Dialogue is one of the best tools for showing — but it can trap writers into telling just as easily as narration.

Dialog Tags

Dialogue tags are used to show who is doing the speaking. That's their only purpose.

Your dialogue tag should be limited to the following:

The following can be used sparingly — they lean toward telling, so keep them limited: replied, answered, asked.

That's about it. As a general rule, any other tags tell instead of show.

Here are some more examples.

Telling

> *"You killed her," David **exclaimed**.*
>
> *"Oh my God, I didn't know," Jane **whispered**.*
>
> *David **growled**, "get out of my office."*

Each one of those tags—exclaimed, whispered, and growled—is telling the reader the emotion of the dialogue.

What should be said instead? Let's rephrase those three lines of dialogue to show instead of tell.

Showing

> *David looked straight at me, unblinking. "You killed her."*
>
> *"Oh my God, I didn't know," Jane said, burying her head in her hands.*
>
> *David stood, turned his back to me, and said, "get out of my office."*

Each version gives the reader something to see — posture, gesture, action — instead of a label.

Often, you don't need dialog tags at all. If you have two people talking back and forth, you only need the tag "said" on the first couple of lines to establish who is doing the speaking. After that, the reader can figure it out unless the order of the speaking changes.

Other tags almost always do the character work the prose should be doing. The better practice is to show the actions, mannerisms, and emotional state in words. Note: strong speaking verbs like bellowed, roared, or whispered work fine as standalone action beats ("He bellowed at the crowd.") – just don't attach them directly to dialogue as tags.

Telling About Dialog

Some authors summarize dialogue rather than writing it out.

Telling

> *David told his mom that he was going to the store.*

This is a form of telling, and dialogue showing the conversation should be used instead.

Showing

> *"Mom," David said. "I'm going to the store."*

Maid and Butler Dialog

The term "Maid and Butler" dialogue means the two characters explain things to each other that both already know. Generally, this is done to inform the reader of something important in the story.

Maid and Butler Dialog

> *"Do you remember that we talked about this last night?"*
>
> *David said, "barely, please remind me."*
>
> *"You told me that you wanted to get out more and spend time with your buddies at the poker game."*
>
> *"Oh, yeah."*

The solution to the Maid and Butler problem is to find a way to deliver the information that creates a genuine need. Put one character in a position where they actually don't know. Let the information surface through action, not explanation.

Dialogue That Tells Through Explanation

One of the subtler forms of telling in dialogue is the explanatory exchange — characters explaining things to each other (and really to the reader) in a way that no real person would.

Telling

> *"As you know, Bob, our company has been losing money for three years because of poor management decisions."*

> *"That's right, and we both know that unless we make major changes in the next quarter, we'll have to shut down."*

No one talks to a colleague this way. Both characters already know these facts. The author is using dialogue as a vehicle to dump information on the reader. This is a form of maid-and-butler dialogue, and it's easy to spot: if both characters already know the information being exchanged, the dialogue exists only to inform the reader.

The fix isn't to cut the information — it may be necessary — but to find a natural way for it to emerge. Put one character in a position where they genuinely don't know. Show a document being read. Let one character discover it through action rather than receiving it through exposition.

Dialogue That Tells Through Emotion-Naming

A second form of telling in dialogue is emotion-naming — characters announcing how they feel rather than behaving in ways that show it.

Telling

> *"I'm furious with you," she said. "I feel completely betrayed."*
>
> *"I understand you're angry. I'm sorry you feel that way."*

Compare that to:

Showing

She set her coffee cup down. "Did you have a good time last night?"

He looked at his phone. "It was fine."

"I'm sure it was."

Nothing is named. The reader fills in everything from tone, timing, and the specific choices — why is she asking about last night? why is he looking at his phone? what does "I'm sure it was" really mean? This is showing through subtext, and it's far more involving than the announced version because the reader is active, making inferences, participating in the scene.

Tags, Beats, and the "Said" Rule in Practice

A practical guide to dialogue mechanics:

Use "said" as your default tag. It disappears. Readers skip over it the way they skip over punctuation. Any other tag — "exclaimed," "gasped," "growled," "hissed" — makes the reader notice the tag, which pulls them out of the dialogue.

When you want to convey how something is said, use an action beat instead of an expressive tag.

Tag (telling)

"Don't come any closer," she whispered.

Action beat (showing)

She stepped back. "Don't come any closer."

The action beat is more vivid because it adds physical behavior to the words. The reader sees her move, hears the words, and draws the conclusion about her state — without being told.

The no-tag approach works when the exchange is clearly back-and-forth between two characters and the rhythm makes it clear who is speaking. Long exchanges can drop tags entirely after the first two lines establish the speakers.

"You knew this whole time."

"I didn't know for certain."

"But you suspected."

"I thought it was possible."

"That's the same thing."

No tags needed. The exchange is clear, and the back-and-forth rhythm carries it. Adding "she said" and "he said" to every line would slow it down without adding anything.

Practice: Strip the Tag

Take three lines of dialogue from your draft that use an expressive tag (exclaimed, snapped, muttered, growled, sighed). Rewrite each one using only "said" plus an action beat. Compare the results.

Showing Using Dialog

One of the best and easiest ways to show is through dialogue.

Telling

> *Bob found out about the affair his wife was having and he was furious.*

That sentence is packed with telling.

Showing

> *"How could you do such a thing?" Bob asked.*
>
> *"I don't know what you're talking about," his wife answered.*
>
> *"Stop playing games! I know. I saw you with him."*
>
> *"Well, you never did satisfy me."*
>
> *"What? That's not what you told me. How dare you!"*

The dialogue shows us everything the one-sentence summary swallowed.

What makes dialogue show rather than tell? It's not just using quotation marks. Telling disguised as dialogue is one of the most common mistakes in fiction — characters explaining things to each other that exist only to inform the reader, or stating their emotions directly in speech.

The difference between dialogue that tells and dialogue that shows comes down to three things: stakes, voice, and what's left unsaid.

Stakes means something has to matter in the exchange. Characters should want something, and either get it or not. Flat dialogue has no stakes — both characters are just delivering information.

Voice means each character sounds like themselves. Characters with distinct voices — different sentence rhythms, different vocabularies, different ways of avoiding or confronting — reveal themselves through speech. When every character sounds the same, the dialogue is doing telling's job: reporting content rather than showing person.

What's left unsaid is often the most powerful element. Characters who say exactly what they mean are boring and unrealistic. Real people deflect, understate, change the subject, or say the opposite of what they mean. Every gap between what a character says and what they want is an opportunity for showing.

Here is dialogue that tells:

Telling

> *"I'm angry at you because you forgot my birthday," Sarah said. "It makes me feel like you don't care about me."*
>
> *"I'm sorry," he said. "I care about you very much. I just have a lot on my mind."*

The characters are explaining their emotional states to each other like reports. No one talks this way. Nothing is revealed that isn't stated.

Here is the same situation rewritten to show:

Showing

She had the cake. She'd bought it herself, a small one, and she'd lit the candle before he got home.

> *"You're home late," she said.*
>
> *"Traffic." He dropped his keys on the counter without looking at her. "Did you eat already?"*
>
> *"I waited." She looked at the cake. He hadn't noticed it yet. "Are you hungry?"*
>
> *"Not really. Long day." He went to the fridge.*

She blew out the candle.

Nothing in the second version announces anger or hurt or carelessness. The reader draws those conclusions from behavior, gesture, and absence. The cake, the waiting, the unnoticed candle — these carry the weight. The dialogue does the work of the scene without announcing what the scene is about.

Dialogue Revealing Character

One of showing's most efficient forms is dialogue that reveals who a character is through how they speak, not what they say.

Telling

James was the kind of person who always had to be right.

Showing

> *"That's not how you pronounce it," James said.*

"Sorry?"

"Quinoa. It's keen-wah." He shook his head slightly. "People always get that wrong."

Nobody had asked.

James is revealed entirely through dialogue and one line of action. The character trait emerges from behavior, not announcement. Three lines of dialogue do more than a full paragraph of description.

The Action Beat

One of the most powerful tools in dialogue is the action beat — a small physical action attached to a line of speech instead of a dialogue tag. Action beats show who is speaking while also revealing emotion, character, or subtext.

Tag (telling the emotion)

"I don't know what you want from me," she said angrily.

Action beat (showing)

She set her glass down on the counter. "I don't know what you want from me."

The action beat tells us she's controlled enough to set the glass down rather than slam it — which is more specific and more interesting than "angrily." It also lets the reader feel the effort of that control.

Action beats work for any emotion. Use them whenever you'd be tempted to reach for an expressive dialogue tag.

Emotions

"Books. It's always easier to tell people that a character is funny rather than attempt to hit the punchline of a joke that character would've said. But if we all simply told, books would cease to exist. And so would empathy. And feeling." – Joyce Rachelle

---

If a novel or story doesn't include emotions, it's boring and lifeless. It doesn't matter whether it's a space opera, a western, a romance, or even a vampire story–emotions are essential to engaging your reader and keeping them reading.

Different emotions require different showing techniques:

ANGER:

> *Subtle: "Her jaw tightened." / "He spoke through clenched teeth."*
>
> *Obvious: "She slammed her fist on the table." / "He kicked the chair across the room."*

FEAR:

Subtle: "Her hand hesitated on the doorknob." / "He found reasons to avoid the basement."

Obvious: "Her heart hammered against her ribs." / "His hands shook as he dialed 911."

LOVE/ATTRACTION:

Subtle: "She found herself saving the last bite for him." / "He remembered exactly how she liked her coffee."

Obvious: "She couldn't stop smiling when he entered the room." / "He studied her face like he was memorizing it."

NERVOUSNESS:

Subtle: "She straightened papers that were already straight." / "He cleared his throat twice."

Obvious: "Sweat beaded on her forehead." / "His leg bounced under the table."

The key is matching the intensity of your showing technique to the intensity of the emotion. Subtle emotions need subtle showing; overwhelming emotions can handle more obvious techniques.

Stating an emotion is telling.

Telling

She was excited.

It's not very interesting, is it?

Showing

She grinned and clapped her hands, "Let's ride the roller coaster again."

There are times when you might be tempted to include both telling and showing in the same sentence.

Telling and Showing

She was happy and smiled.

The word "happy" is telling because it gives the reader a conclusion about her emotional state, while "smiled" is showing because it's something that can be seen or perceived.

Showing

She smiled, showing off her pure white teeth, and clapped her hands. "Let's ride the roller coaster again."

Sometimes the telling part isn't even needed.

Telling and Showing

Bill was angry, glared at me and held up his fist.

Let's look at the same sentence without telling.

Showing

Bill glared at me and held up his fist.

The emotion "angry" isn't even needed. The writing which shows body language demonstrates the emotion of anger just fine.

Body Language

Use body language to show emotion. For example, to show anger a character can raise their fist, glare, or even scream. To show a controlling character, have them interrupt mid-sentence, rearrange objects someone else just placed, or speak for another person.

Expressions

Use facial expressions to show emotion.

Telling

Bill was puzzled at her response.

Showing

Bill frowned and looked to the ceiling. He rolled his eyes as if to ask for help from the heavens.

Physical Responses

When a person experiences emotion, there are physical responses of some kind. When they become angry, their face turns red, their brow furrows, and they narrow their eyes.

Telling

She was afraid for her life.

Showing

She reached into her purse but dropped it on the ground. She picked it up, her hands trembling, and fumbled around until she found the money.

Dialog

Sometimes the best way to show emotion is to write some dialogue.

Telling

Dana was angry at Sam.

Showing

Dana slammed her fist on the table. "Damn you," she said. "Why do you always act so stupid? Did you have to embarrass me like that?"

Thoughts

Another way to show emotion is to show the thoughts of your characters.

Telling

Dana was enjoying the play.

Showing

Her eyes riveted on the play, Dana smiled. Now that's great acting, she thought. Why don't we see more of that kind of performance today?

Senses

Your characters have many senses or ways to perceive the physical universe. Use them all in your writing to describe emotions.

Telling

Their lips met, and they kissed.

Showing

He gently pressed his lips against hers, and he tasted the faint flavor of cherry from her lip balm.

More About Emotions

Ask yourself some questions about the characters in your scene.

How does the street smell — exhaust, food carts, rain on concrete? When a character hugs another, is there the smell of cigarette smoke? When your character runs across the street, does a car have to slam on its brakes with a screeching sound? How does your character feel while sleeping under a blanket — warm, or does it fail to cover her feet?

Let the scene itself guide you. What would a person in this situation actually feel in their body? Start there.

Weak

Dana licked her lips.

Stronger

Dana licked her lips. Where is he? Dana thought. He said he was going to be here at 9.

In the first example, it's good that she's licking her lips, but that could mean she's anxious, hungry, or thirsty. We can make this stronger by combining two techniques–body language and internal thoughts–to clarify that she's anxious.

Don't overuse the same emotional indicators throughout your story and mix them up for different characters. It would be kind of strange if all your characters raised their fist whenever they were angry. You can use thoughts for one character, dialogue for another, and facial expressions for a third, and then change it around for each character as the story progresses. After all, people act differently when they experience emotions so why shouldn't your characters?

I recommend you pick up a copy of *The Emotion Thesaurus*. This book lists the body language, thoughts, and responses for each of 75 emotions. It's one of the most practical reference books any fiction writer can own.

All the books in the series that are useful include:

Other books in the series worth having: Emotion Amplifiers, The Emotion Thesaurus, The Negative Trait Thesaurus, The

Positive Trait Thesaurus, The Emotional Wound Thesaurus, The Rural Setting Thesaurus, and The Urban Setting Thesaurus.

Each of these books is a practical reference for finding specific ways to show character traits and emotions rather than telling them.

Practice: Show Without Naming

Find a sentence in your draft that names an emotion (angry, sad, afraid, proud, ashamed, excited). Rewrite that moment — as many sentences as you need — without using the emotion's name, any synonym for it, or any filter word. Use only physical behavior and what the character notices. If you don't have a draft: pick one emotion and write a paragraph showing it in a character without naming it once.

Avoid Info Dumps

An information dump is exactly what it sounds like. This is the act of dumping data on the reader. The author believes the information is necessary, but instead of weaving it into the story, throws it at the reader all at once.

Every time a movie starts with narration, the script writer is doing an information dump.

In *Star Wars*, that scroll of text at the beginning, before the movie even starts, is an information dump. That's not storytelling, it's front-loading exposition.

Sometimes the writer feels the need to tell some back story (past events) to set the scene. Rather than front-load the backstory, it's better to either skip it entirely or weave it into the narrative as events unfold.

If you've ever read novels such as *Lord of the Rings* or *Dune*, you'll notice that there is a phenomenal amount of exposition dumped on the reader before the story even starts. In *Lord of the Rings*, the entire history of middle earth is told, and in *Dune* the author feels it is necessary to bring the reader up to date on much of the history of mankind since space travel began.

It's much better to reveal the back story as the main story progresses and only inform the readers of things as and when necessary. Another option is to write a prologue, which the reader can skip if they wish.

World building

Science fiction and fantasy tend to use large information dumps because the author feels it is necessary to set the stage. Again, there is no need to explain the why's and wherefores of the world that you've designed. You don't need to tell your readers about the politics of your planet, or how the ecology has changed, or why alien beings exist in Los Angeles.

Just weave it into the story. Your readers will notice the difference.

Look at one of the most popular television series of all time, *Game of Thrones*. The first season is a masterclass in world-building without information dumps.

Instead, we find out details about the world as the story progresses. We learn about the importance of dragons in a conversation between two characters. The concept of the game of thrones is introduced by showing us an empty throne, and then that is backed up a few times with some dialogue.

The insanity of certain characters is shown by having them act insane. Other emotions such as fear, hate, cowardice and so on are shown quite expertly.

The best way to build your world is to assume that your readers and your characters already know all about it. Write as though the world is simply the world.

Your readers know nothing when the story opens. Dole out information as the story demands it. Trust the story to deliver context when it's needed.

How Info Dumps Happen

Info dumps almost always occur at beginnings. The beginning of a novel, the beginning of a chapter, the beginning of a scene. The writer feels anxious — the reader doesn't know enough yet

— and the anxiety produces explanation. Before anything happens, the writer explains the situation.

The solution isn't to write less backstory. It's to deliver it differently: woven into action, triggered by need, doled out in fragments.

Here is a scene opening that dumps backstory:

Info Dump

Sarah had grown up in this town and hated it. Her parents had divorced when she was eight, and her father had left for Denver, where he'd started a new family. Her mother had stayed, working at the diner on Route 9 for twenty-three years. Sarah had left for college and come back twice — once for her grandmother's funeral, once when her mother had surgery. Both times she'd promised herself she wouldn't stay long. Now she was parking in front of the house she'd grown up in, called back because her mother had fallen and couldn't manage alone.

That paragraph contains a lot of true and useful information. It's also inert — nothing is happening except information transfer.

Here is the same information woven into scene:

Woven

Sarah parked in front of the house and turned off the engine. The diner sign was still lit at the end of the block. Twenty-three years her mother had walked to that sign and back. She'd done it the morning of the divorce. She'd done it the week Sarah left for college. She was still doing it the day she fell.

Sarah got out of the car.

The second version doesn't explain the backstory — it implies it. We understand the duration and weight of her mother's life in that town through one concrete detail (the diner sign, twenty-three years). The divorce is present as a shadow. Sarah's history of leaving and coming back is in the economy of her actions. The reader does more work, and the reward is that the scene feels lived-in rather than reported.

The Woven Backstory Rule

When you have backstory to deliver, ask: what is happening in the present scene that could naturally trigger a memory, comparison, or reflection that contains the information?

A character walking into an old house can register details that imply history. A character reuniting with someone can notice what's changed — which implies what was. A character handling an object can remember when they last held it. Every present action is an opportunity to surface the past without stopping to explain it.

The reader does not need the backstory upfront. They need just enough to understand what's at stake in the moment they're in. Give them the rest as the story earns it.

How to Introduce Technical Detail Without Dumping

The technique is the same as with backstory: let the story's action create the need for the information, then give just enough to serve that moment.

Info dump

The Kepler-7 drive worked by creating a resonance bubble around the ship, bending local space-time so that the effective distance between two points was reduced. The theoretical basis had been developed by Dr. Amara Singh in 2089, building on work that had been done at MIT's Advanced Physics Lab since 2071. The drive required seventeen minutes of spin-up time and produced a significant gravitational signature that could be detected up to four light-hours away.

Woven

"Seventeen minutes," Chen said. He didn't look away from the scanner. "If they're tracking our spin-up signature, they already know we're here."

"Then we move fast." She hit the initiation sequence. The drive began its low hum, the kind that lived in your back teeth rather than your ears.

In the second version, the reader learns what they need in the moment they need it: the drive takes seventeen minutes and produces a detectable signature. Everything else — the theoretical history, the lab origins — doesn't matter to this scene. Trust the story to create future moments that can deliver future details.

Technology

Don't do technical information dumps. That's where you tell your readers all about a subject that is pertinent to your story.

If you're writing a romance in ancient Egypt, your readers don't need to know how the pyramids were built, or about the complexities of Egyptian politics.

In a space opera, it's not necessary to describe how faster than light travel works or the intricacies of repairing a spaceship in port. Few readers will care, and those who don't will stop reading.

Instead, seed technical details into the story as events require them. Keep them unobtrusive and specific.

Remember that a novel is a story, not a technical manual.

Emotions

In real life, people don't talk on and on about other people's emotions.

> "Why are you acting so weird? Yesterday you kept looking away from me. You have something to hide? I mean, you couldn't meet my eyes. It was strange."

This is telling hidden inside dialogue. One character is delivering an emotional report. There's no scene, no tension — just information.

Instead, let the scene carry the emotion — physical reactions, dialogue, the character's internal response.

Practice: Weave the Backstory

Find a passage in your draft where you've stopped the story to explain backstory. Rewrite it as a scene in which the backstory surfaces through what a character notices, how they react, or what they do — without stopping the forward action. If you don't have a draft: write a scene in which two characters meet for the first time and one of them has significant history with the location. In 150 words, convey that history through detail and behavior, not explanation.

Use All The Senses

When I was in school, the textbooks said there are five senses.

The standard five are sight, hearing, taste, touch, and smell.

As with many things taught in school, this is not the whole truth. Humans have many other senses than just these five.

Your vestibular system senses gravity and acceleration. That's not in the standard five.

Your body senses acceleration and deceleration — the lurch when a car brakes, the pressure of takeoff.

You can have a sense of direction. Some people navigate without a map or compass — they simply feel the cardinal points.

What about feelings of low blood sugar? Wouldn't that be a sense? Doesn't your body tell you that you're having low or high blood sugar?

Other senses include balance, the tilt of the head, the stretching of muscles and tendons, the level of oxygen in the bloodstream, pressure, itch, temperature, pain, thirst, hunger, time, and proprioception — knowing where your body parts are relative to each other.

Researchers identify at least 20 distinct human senses beyond the traditional five.

In paranormal or speculative fiction, you can add invented senses — the ability to perceive ghosts, read emotions, or sense another dimension.

When you're showing your readers something, draw from multiple senses to pull readers deeper into the scene.

Showing

> *As I walked along the garden path, I breathed deeply, smelling the scent of pine with just a hint of orange blossom. I stopped and listened; there was a low toned buzzing noise to my right. Turning my head slowly, I spied a tiny hummingbird hovering in front of a blue flower. I smiled and continued my walk.*

The passage uses smell, sound, and sight to put readers inside the character's experience.

When you're writing a passage in your story, imagine the scene using all your senses. What does your character see? What do they smell? How does the food that they're eating taste? What is in front of your character? What does it look like? What color is it? How far away is it?

By mixing up the senses in your writing, you add depth to your story and make it more interesting for your readers. The right combination of senses makes a scene feel lived-in.

For example, if your character is walking through a forest, imagine the plants and animals all around. Imagine the trees, bushes, flowers, birds, bees, pinecones, and so on. Imagine the color of the sky and the weather, the temperature of the air and the speed of the wind, and the smell of the flowers or the rotting trash that someone threw out of their car window.

If you are writing a book about flying in a spaceship, you might be concerned with the sense of gravity and inertia and its effects on the human body. As a spaceship maneuvers, the people inside will feel shifts from acceleration and deceleration and changes in direction. Adding these to your narrative adds depth to your story.

Here's how to effectively use each sense:

SIGHT: Don't just describe what something looks like—show what the character notices based on their emotional state.

EMOTIONAL: "The red roses looked like drops of blood on white snow." (fearful character)

NEUTRAL: "Red roses dotted the white garden." (calm character)

SOUND: Use sound to create mood and reveal character reactions.

"The grandfather clock's ticking filled the silence between them."

"Somewhere upstairs, a floorboard groaned."

TOUCH: Include temperature, texture, weight, and pressure.

"The doorknob was ice-cold under her sweaty palm."

"The letter felt heavier than it should have."

SMELL: The most memory-triggering sense—use it to establish setting and evoke emotion.

"The hospital smell of disinfectant and floor wax brought back memories of her father's last days."

TASTE: Often overlooked but powerful for emotional moments.

"Fear tasted like copper pennies in her mouth."

"The coffee had gone bitter and cold, like her mood."

Don't use all five senses in every scene, choose the one or two that best serve your story's emotional purpose.

Choosing the Right Sense for the Scene

Knowing the senses exist is one thing. Knowing which one to reach for in a given moment is craft. Each sense carries a different emotional weight, triggers different memories, and creates a different kind of intimacy with the reader.

Smell is the most underused and the most powerful. It bypasses conscious processing and lands directly in the emotional and memory centers of the brain — which is why the smell of your grandmother's kitchen can return you to childhood in an instant. In fiction, smell creates setting faster than any other sense and it carries emotional history. A character who smells their late father's aftershave on a stranger doesn't need to explain what they feel.

Telling

The old house reminded her of her childhood.

Showing

The smell hit her first — Murphy Oil Soap and something underneath it, something like her father's study, pipe tobacco ground into old wood. She stood in the doorway without going in.

Smell placed her in the scene. Nothing else was needed.

Sound establishes presence and danger. We hear things we can't see. A sound behind you in an empty parking garage does something to the body that a visual description of the same garage cannot. Use sound to create the sense of a world existing beyond the frame of what the character can directly observe.

Telling

The house felt empty and eerie.

Showing

> *She called out. Her voice came back wrong — too flat, no echo. She called again. Somewhere above her, a pipe knocked once and went quiet.*

Touch is the most intimate sense and the most overlooked. Texture, weight, temperature, and pressure are physical facts that ground readers in a body. When a character's hands shake so badly they can't hold a cup, the reader feels it. When someone grips a railing to keep standing, the reader grips it with them.

Taste appears in moments that demand it — meals, kisses, blood, fear. "Fear tasted like copper pennies" works because it's unexpected and precise. Don't invent taste sensations for scenes where they don't belong, but when a moment calls for taste, use it fully.

Sight is the default sense for most writers and therefore the least surprising. Don't describe everything visually. Your readers already live in a visual world. The other senses are the ones that pull them somewhere new.

Layering Senses Without Overloading

The goal is not to use all the senses in every paragraph. The goal is to find the one or two senses that make a particular scene vivid and press on those.

A scene set in a hospital operating theater might use: the sharp cold of the room, the smell of antiseptic and something beneath it the character can't name, the hiss and click of machines, the weight of the gown. That's four senses — but each one is chosen because it does something specific. Each one adds a layer of reality that sight alone can't deliver.

Contrast that with a scene set on a first date. You might use: the smell of wine and garlic from the kitchen, the ambient noise of conversation that makes it hard to hear, the roughness of the paper tablecloth under her fingernails while she tries to seem relaxed. Three senses, three distinct emotional notes: anticipation, effort, anxiety.

When you sit down to write a scene, ask yourself which senses are available to the POV character at that moment, and which ones carry the emotional charge of what the scene is about. Start there. You don't need all of them. You need the right ones.

A Note on the Body's Interior Senses

The body's internal senses — proprioception, the vestibular system, hunger, the stretch of a muscle — are particularly useful for showing emotional states that characters can't or won't name.

A character in shock doesn't feel terror. They feel their legs not responding the way they should. They feel disconnected from their own hands. They feel suddenly very cold.

A character who is deeply anxious feels their stomach, the tension across their shoulders, the slight dizziness from breathing too fast without realizing it.

Telling

She was terrified.

Showing

> *She couldn't feel her hands. She looked at them — they were shaking — but the sensation of holding the railing had gone somewhere else. Her breath was coming in short pulls. She made herself slow it down.*

The interior body is an emotional barometer. When a character's emotion is too large to name, go to the body. The body always knows first.

Practice: One Sense at a Time

Take a scene from your draft and identify which sense dominates the description. Rewrite two or three key sentences using a different sense entirely. Note whether the scene's atmosphere changes and which sense serves the moment better. If you don't have a draft: write the same moment (a character arriving somewhere unfamiliar at night) three times — once using only sound, once only smell, once only touch.

Showing Setting and Atmosphere

A setting described is not the same as a setting felt. Most writers know how to describe a place — they list its features, note its dimensions, catalogue its details. Fewer writers know how to make a place feel like something: oppressive, alive, hostile, welcoming, charged with menace or memory.

The difference is the same as the difference between telling and showing anywhere else. Describing a place gives readers information. Showing a place creates an experience.

Setting Through the POV Character's State

A place doesn't feel like anything in isolation. It feels like something to a specific person in a specific emotional state. The most powerful way to show setting is to filter it through your POV character's consciousness — not as a neutral tour guide describing what's there, but as a person whose current state shapes what they notice and how they interpret it.

Telling

The old house felt sinister and unwelcoming.

Showing

The floorboards gave slightly under each step, like something beneath them was uncertain. The smell was old paper and something sweeter underneath — not food, not flowers. She couldn't place it and didn't want to.

The first version tells the reader what conclusion to reach. The second puts the reader in the house with a character whose unease shapes every detail she registers. The sweet smell she can't identify and doesn't want to identify is doing more atmospheric work than any adjective.

Telling

The city felt alive and electric.

Showing

Even at this hour, the street had a current running through it — bodies moving with purpose, the bass thrum from a bar two blocks down, a man selling coffee from a cart who called out to everyone who passed and meant it. She hadn't felt this anonymous in years. It was a relief.

The atmosphere is entirely in the details chosen and the one line of character interiority at the end. We know it's night. We know it's a city. We feel what it's like to be there for this particular character.

Choosing the Details That Carry the Atmosphere

Not all details are equal. The goal is to find the details that do double or triple duty — that establish physical reality while also carrying emotional weight and revealing character.

For a scene set in a decaying mansion, you could describe peeling wallpaper, dusty chandeliers, and cracked plaster.

These are accurate. They're also generic — any decaying mansion would have them.

More specific details create more specific atmosphere:

Telling

The house was in disrepair, clearly abandoned for years.

Showing

A child's drawing was still taped to the kitchen wall, yellowed and curling at the corners. Whoever had left had left quickly — a coffee cup sat on the counter, just a brown ring now, the residue of whatever was in it gone to evaporation sometime in the past decade.

The child's drawing and the coffee cup are not generic decay. They imply a specific departure, a specific life interrupted. They create a feeling that goes beyond "the house was old."

Setting as Active Pressure

In strong fiction, setting isn't backdrop — it's pressure. The place exerts force on the characters. Heat makes people short-tempered. A cramped room escalates tension. An open landscape can produce vulnerability or freedom depending on who's crossing it and why.

When you write setting, ask: what does this place want to do to my character? Then show the place doing it.

Telling

The desert was harsh and unforgiving.

Showing

By midday, thinking took effort. Her thoughts arrived in fragments and she had to hold them deliberately, the way you hold something slippery. She'd stopped conserving water two hours ago. That probably meant something.

Telling

The party was glamorous and overwhelming.

Showing

The noise was the first thing — not loud music but dozens of simultaneous conversations, all pitched slightly too high, the specific frequency of people performing having a good time. She accepted a glass of something from a tray and found a wall.

Setting changes. Track it.

One of the most effective uses of setting is to show how a character's relationship to a place changes as the scene develops. A room that feels neutral at the start of a tense conversation can feel airless and close by the end. A familiar kitchen can feel alien the morning after a death in the family.

You don't need to describe the room again. One or two registered details — the way the light looks now, something that didn't seem relevant before that suddenly is — can carry the shift. The setting becomes a record of the character's changing internal state.

Practice: The Same Room, Different Character

Find a scene in your draft where a character enters or occupies a space. Rewrite the description of that space filtered through a version of the character with a completely different emotional state — what would they notice then that they don't notice now? If you don't have a draft: write the same room twice, once from a character who has just received good news, once from a character who has just received bad news. Physical detail only. Don't name their emotional states.

Showing Through Point of View

Point of view is not just a technical choice about who narrates. It shapes everything that gets shown — what details a character notices, how they interpret what they see, and what the reader is allowed to know. Understanding how POV controls showing is one of the most practical skills in this book.

What POV Controls

POV determines what your narrator can know, see, hear, and reveal. But it also determines something less obvious: what details a character notices, and what those noticed details reveal about the character.

Two people walk into the same room. A chef notices the quality of the cookware. A detective notices the door to the back room is slightly ajar. A grieving widow notices that her husband's chair is still pushed back from the table, the way he always left it. Same room. Three completely different scenes.

The detail a POV character notices is never neutral. It tells the reader who that character is, what they care about, and how they see the world. Choosing the right noticed detail is one of the most efficient forms of showing available to you.

Telling

Elena was a careful person who worried about everything.

Showing (through POV)

> *Elena checked the stove twice before she left. She'd already checked it once, knew she'd checked it, but the knowing didn't help.*

Nothing has been stated about Elena's character. The reader learns it through what she notices and does — which is a function of whose head we're in.

The Three POV Modes

First person puts the narrator inside the story as a participant. The "I" character filters everything. First person creates the most immediate intimacy, but it's also the most constrained — you can only show what this one character can directly observe or know.

Third person limited stays close to one character's perspective — their observations, thoughts, and sensory experience — while using "he" or "she" rather than "I." This is the dominant mode of contemporary commercial fiction because it offers nearly the same intimacy as first person while allowing slightly more narrative flexibility.

Third person omniscient allows the narrator to know everything about any character and to move freely between perspectives. It's common in classic literature and certain types of epic fiction, but it requires discipline. The temptation with omniscient is to tell readers what characters think and feel rather than showing it — you can know everyone's inner life, which can make it easy to just report it. Omniscient narrators who show rather than tell work hard to stay in scene, stay specific, and let readers draw conclusions.

POV and Scene Restriction

Whatever POV you're using, restrict what you show to what your POV character can genuinely perceive and know at that moment in the story.

This isn't just a rule about accuracy. It's a showing technique. When your POV character doesn't know something, readers feel the limitation — and that tension is one of the most powerful tools in fiction.

In a scene where a protagonist is hiding and listening to a conversation in the next room, the protagonist can hear voices but can't see faces. They can make guesses about emotional tone, but those guesses might be wrong. The reader is in the dark alongside the character. That shared uncertainty creates suspense no omniscient description of the scene could generate.

Telling (omniscient, over-explained)

From his hiding place, David listened. In the next room, Sandra was telling Marcus about the money, and Marcus was furious, though he was hiding it well.

Showing (restricted POV)

> *David pressed his back to the wall. He could hear Sandra's voice — too steady, the way she got when she was nervous — and a man's responses, short, clipped. A chair scraped. Something hit the table, not hard, but deliberate.*

The second version doesn't tell us Marcus is furious. David can't know that from a wall away. The reader hears what David hears and draws the same uncertain conclusions.

Head-Hopping and Why It Breaks the Contract

Head-hopping is the term for switching POV mid-scene without signaling the shift — being inside Character A's perspective, then suddenly inside Character B's. It's one of the most common POV errors and one of the most damaging to the reader's experience, because every time it happens, the showing breaks down into telling.

When you're in Character A's head and you suddenly tell us what Character B is thinking or feeling, you're telling the reader something from outside the scene's established perspective. The reader loses their footing — they no longer know whose experience they're inside.

The fix is simple: pick one POV character per scene and stay there. If the scene requires you to know what another character is thinking, find a way to externalize it — a look on their face, a change in their voice, a gesture that the POV character can observe and interpret.

Put yourself fully in the eyes, ears, body, and mind of your POV character. Show only what they can perceive. Everything else is either inferred, observed, or left unknown — and that unknown is often the most powerful showing of all.

Practice: Limit the View

Find a scene in your draft where your POV character knows more than they could realistically perceive in that moment. Rewrite it restricting the POV strictly to what they can see, hear, or sense from their physical position. What uncertainty does the restriction create? If you don't have a draft: rewrite this as a full paragraph from the POV of a character who can only hear: "The two men argued in the next room."

Add Some Conflict

Conflict in dialogue does double duty — it reveals character and avoids telling by showing emotions in action. But conflict in fiction is broader than argument. It's any friction between what a character wants and what they're getting. Scene-level conflict is what separates a scene that has things happening from a scene that matters.

The Flat Exchange Problem

Here's the most common failure in beginner dialogue:

Telling

> *"How's the weather?" Tom asked.*
>
> *"It's going to rain," Jill replied.*

Tom said, "that's nice."

The author has embedded telling inside the dialogue. The reader is simply being told that it's going to rain. No one has a stake in the exchange. Nothing changes.

With Conflict and Voice

> *"How's the weather?" Tom asked.*
>
> *"The weatherman screwed up again. I thought it was supposed to be sunny, and I wanted to wear my bathing suit, but it looks like it's going to rain," Jill replied. "And I didn't even bring my umbrella. Stupid weatherman."*
>
> *"That's too bad. Does the weatherman ever get it right?"*

The second version is more alive — it adds conflict and voice to what was a flat exchange. Jill has opinions, frustration, a ruined plan. Tom is gently needling her. We learn something about both of them.

Subtext: What They Don't Say

The most powerful conflicts in fiction happen beneath the surface. Characters rarely say exactly what they mean. Two people who have just had a fight don't talk about the fight — they talk about where to have dinner, and every word about dinner is about the fight.

Two characters, the morning after an argument:

Telling

> *They were still angry at each other from the night before and breakfast was uncomfortable.*

Showing

> *"Coffee?" she said.*
>
> *"I can make it."*
>
> *"I already made it."*

He looked at the pot. "Thanks."

> *She sat down with her cup and opened her laptop. He poured a mug and stood by the window. Outside, someone was mowing a lawn. Neither of them said anything.*

Nothing about the argument is mentioned. The argument is in every word. This is subtext — the gap between what characters say and what they mean.

To write subtext, know what your characters actually want in the scene. Then have them talk around it. They bring it up sideways. They mention it and drop it. They almost say it and don't.

Conflict as Character Revelation

Every conflict reveals character because conflict forces choice. How a character responds to friction — with aggression, deflection, humor, silence, honesty — tells you who they are more efficiently than any description.

Telling

Mike was the kind of person who didn't back down from a fight.

Showing

> *"I said move your car." The man was a head taller than Mike, gym-built, jaw set.*
>
> *Mike looked at his own car, then at the space the man was gesturing toward. Plenty of room. He'd checked twice.*
>
> *"It's a legal spot," Mike said.*
>
> *"Move it."*
>
> *"No."*

You know Mike now. You know him in a way that no amount of description could deliver, because you watched him make a choice under pressure.

Scene Conflict vs. Dialogue Conflict

Conflict doesn't have to live in dialogue. A character can be in conflict with the environment, with time, with their own body, with a task.

Telling

She was nervous about performing.

Showing

> *She stood in the wings with her sheet music, the paper damp from her palms. She'd played this piece five hundred times. Her fingers ran through the opening bars against her thigh — there, fine, perfect — but her heart was going too fast and the house lights were still on and people were still finding their seats and she had no idea when they'd dim and she needed them to dim.*

No one is arguing. The conflict is between what the character needs (stillness, readiness) and what the world is giving her (chaos, waiting, her own body). Conflict doesn't require another person. It requires want, obstacle, and pressure.

The Conflict Checklist

Before you write a scene, ask: what does my character want? What's in the way? What are the stakes if they don't get it? If you can't answer all three, the scene will feel flat no matter how well you write it. Conflict isn't what makes a scene dramatic. It's what makes a scene exist.

Practice: The Argument About Nothing

Find a scene in your draft where two characters argue or have a tense exchange. Identify what the argument is really about underneath. Now rewrite it so the real subject is never named — only the surface complaint. If you don't have a draft: write a 150-word scene in which two characters argue about something trivial while the real conflict is something neither will say.

When Should You Tell?

None of this means you should never tell. The best writers tell all the time — deliberately, strategically, and with full awareness of what telling does that showing can't.

The mistake isn't telling. The mistake is telling when you should be showing, or showing when you should be telling. The skill is knowing the difference.

What Telling Does That Showing Can't

Showing puts readers inside a moment and stretches it. Telling compresses time and moves readers from one important moment to the next. A novel told entirely in showing would be unreadable — every trip to the grocery store would take thirty pages. Telling gives the story its skeleton. Showing gives it flesh.

There are five situations where telling is usually the right choice.

The first is transition. When time passes between scenes and nothing significant happens in that gap, tell it briefly.

Telling (appropriate)

Three weeks passed. Neither of them called.

This single sentence covers three weeks in six words. Showing those three weeks of silence would kill the pacing. The reader doesn't need to live through the silence — they need to know it happened and feel its weight. Telling does that better.

The second is summary. When a series of similar events happens repeatedly over time, summarize rather than dramatizing each one.

Telling (appropriate)

> *For the rest of that summer, she drove to the lake every morning and sat there until noon. She stopped explaining it to herself.*

This covers a summer in two sentences. The emotional truth is in those sentences. You don't need thirty lake scenes. You need the reader to feel that she did this repeatedly, and that whatever drove her there settled into habit.

The third is backstory. Readers sometimes need context to understand why a present moment matters. The rule isn't "never give backstory." The rule is "don't dump it." Woven in as brief summary — a sentence or two, grounded in the present scene — backstory is telling used well.

The fourth is minor characters. Not every person in your story deserves a scene. A taxi driver who appears for three paragraphs can be told in a sentence or two of quick characterization without slowing the story to dramatize an insignificant encounter.

The fifth is pace acceleration. When you need to move quickly — building toward a climax, creating urgency, or recovering momentum after a slow scene — telling speeds things up. Short, declarative sentences that tell the reader what's happening can drive a scene forward in a way that detailed showing sometimes can't.

The Permission to Tell

Many beginning writers, after learning show-don't-tell, become afraid of any telling at all. They describe conversations that could be summarized in two sentences. They dramatize transitions that don't need dramatizing. They show events that don't carry enough weight to justify being lived through in full.

The result is prose that exhausts readers, not because it's bad but because it gives everything equal weight. When everything is shown, nothing stands out.

The rhythm of fiction is alternation — showing and telling in balance. A long, closely rendered scene has more impact when it follows a section of compressed narrative. Telling is what makes the showing land.

The Test

When you're not sure whether to show or tell a moment, ask yourself two questions. First: does the reader need to experience this moment, or just know it happened? If they need to experience it — if the scene depends on feeling it from the inside — show it. If knowing it happened is enough, tell it.

Second: is this moment one of the three or four most important in this chapter? If no, consider telling it. Save your showing for what matters most.

Telling in the Character's Voice

There's a particular kind of telling that works better than either pure narration or pure showing: telling filtered through the POV character's voice. When the character's perspective and personality shape the summary, it becomes almost as intimate as showing.

Compare these two:

Neutral telling

Tom had grown up in the house. He knew every room.

Character-voiced telling

> *Tom had grown up in that house, which meant he knew which floorboards to avoid and which drawers had stopped working in 1987 and exactly how loud you had to shut the back door to keep it from drifting open in the night. He knew the house the way you can only know a place you've hated for years.*

The second is still telling — nothing is dramatized, nothing is shown in real time. But the character's voice has made it specific, and that specificity makes it alive. This is telling at its best: efficient, purposeful, and saturated with the character's particular way of seeing the world.

Tell what doesn't need to be shown. Show what does. Know which is which.

Practice: Tell It Right

Take a transition in your current draft where you currently have a scene that could be summarized. Rewrite it as a single sentence of telling. Then write a second version as two sentences of character-voiced telling. Compare which creates the better rhythm for what comes after.

Interiority: The Character's Inner World

Every story lives in two places: the world outside the character and the world inside. You've learned to show the outside —

actions, dialogue, sensory detail. But the inside is where readers fall in love with characters. Interiority is the character's inner life: thoughts, feelings, realizations, memories, and the ongoing commentary a person runs in their own head. It's also the most misunderstood territory in fiction, because it sits right on the border between showing and telling — and crossing to the wrong side is easy.

The good news: when you handle interiority well, it does more work per word than almost any other technique.

The Filtering Word Problem

The most common interiority mistake is the filtering word. A filtering word stands between the reader and the character's experience.

Telling

She realized she had forgotten her keys.

The word "realized" filters the experience. It tells us that a realization happened rather than putting us inside the realization. Other filtering words include: knew, thought, felt, noticed, saw, heard, wondered, understood, remembered. They push readers out of the character's head and into the narrator's report.

Showing

> *Her hand found only fabric in her pocket. She stood at the door, staring at the lock. The spare was at her mother's. Thirty minutes away.*

No filtering word. The reader experiences the realization as it happens, beat by beat. The thought isn't explained — it unfolds.

This is the core principle: don't report a thought. Enact it.

Telling

He understood that the meeting had not gone well.

Showing

> *He loosened his tie in the elevator. Seventeen floors. On the fourth, he realized he'd been holding his breath since the handshakes. Nobody had made eye contact when they left.*

The second version doesn't name the understanding. It shows the evidence that produces it, then lets the reader draw the same conclusion the character is drawing.

Three Ways to Render Thought

You have three tools for showing interiority, and each creates a different distance between reader and character.

The first is tagged thought, where you attach a dialogue-like tag: She thought, He wondered, I told myself. This is the most distanced form. Use it sparingly, when you need to establish clearly that a character is reflecting rather than acting.

She thought about calling him. She didn't.

The second is italicized thought, rendered as if the reader is hearing the character's voice directly, usually in present tense even if the surrounding narrative is past tense.

> *She reached for the phone. Don't. He'll think you're desperate. She put it back.*

This is more immediate than tagged thought. The reader hears the character's actual voice, not a report of it. It works well for short, sharp internal reactions.

The third is free indirect discourse, the most powerful and the most difficult. Here, the character's thought is embedded directly into the narrative without tags or italics. The narrator's voice and the character's voice merge.

> *She reached for the phone. He'd think she was desperate. She put it back.*

The sentence "He'd think she was desperate" exists in a strange space — it's not clearly narration or clearly thought. It reads as both simultaneously. The reader is inside the character's head without any signal that they've entered. This is the technique that makes great literary fiction feel intimate without ever breaking the surface of the prose.

Most published commercial and literary fiction relies heavily on free indirect discourse. When you read a novel and feel like you know a character from the inside, this is usually how that intimacy was created.

The Over-Explanation Trap

Beginning writers often explain what a character's thoughts mean.

Telling

> *She smiled at him, but it wasn't a real smile. She was performing happiness she didn't feel, hoping he wouldn't notice the sadness underneath.*

The second sentence is the mistake. "She was performing happiness she didn't feel" tells the reader what to conclude from the false smile. Trust the false smile to do its job.

Showing

> *She smiled at him. She could feel the effort in it, the particular tension in her cheeks.*

Now the reader and the character notice the same thing at the same time. No explanation needed.

The rule: if you've shown it, don't explain it. Your job is to create the experience of the thought, not to summarize it afterward.

Interiority Reveals Character

Interiority is one of your most powerful character tools because it shows the gap between what a character does and what they actually think. That gap is where personality lives.

A character who comforts a grieving friend while internally counting the minutes until they can leave is more interesting than a character who simply comforts a friend. The action is kind. The thought is human.

Telling

David helped his brother move, even though he didn't want to.

Showing

> *David carried the third box up three flights and set it down in the kitchen. His brother was already back downstairs. David looked at the stack by the door — eleven more. He could hear a game starting from somewhere down the hall. He picked up the fourth box.*

Nothing tells us David would rather be watching the game. We know it because we're inside the effort it takes him to keep going. That's character through interiority.

Keeping It Clean

A few practical rules. First, stay in one POV character's head per scene — interiority that jumps between characters is disorienting. Second, interiority in action scenes should be brief. When the pace is fast, long passages of thought will kill momentum. A single sharp internal sentence is usually enough. Third, internal monologue can become self-indulgent. If your character's thoughts go on for three paragraphs without anything happening, you've probably shifted from showing to telling about emotions.

Interiority done well is invisible. The reader doesn't think: this character is thinking. They simply think along with the character, as if the thoughts are their own.

That's the goal.

Practice: Remove the Filter

Find five sentences in your draft that contain a filter word (realized, noticed, felt, thought, heard, saw). Rewrite each one without the filter word so the reader experiences the perception directly. Read the two versions aloud and note the difference in immediacy.

Showing Character Change

Character change is the engine of most fiction. A character who is the same person at the end of the story as they were at the beginning has not had a story — they've had a series of events. The arc, the transformation, the lesson learned or refused — this is what readers stay for.

But character change is one of the most commonly told elements in all of fiction. Writers announce it rather than demonstrate it.

Telling

By the end of the summer, Daniel had changed. He was no longer the angry, closed-off person he had been when he arrived.

Showing is the only way this works. The reader must see the person Daniel was, observe the forces that act on him, and then see — in concrete behavior, choice, and response — a person who acts differently than he would have before.

The Before Must Be Shown, Not Told

You cannot show change if you have only told the starting point. If the reader knows Daniel is closed-off because the narration told them he was closed-off, watching him open up carries no weight. They haven't seen the closedness. They have no baseline.

The beginning of a character arc requires showing the behavior that will change — not describing the character trait that will change. Show the character acting in the way they'll stop acting. Show the choice they make that they'll later regret or learn from.

Telling

Elena had always pushed people away when they got too close.

Showing (establishing the before)

"I should go," Elena said, even though it was early, even though she didn't want to. She was already reaching for her coat. Michael looked at her the way he'd looked at her before — patient, waiting for the explanation that never came. She didn't give him one. She never did.

Now when Elena stays — when she reaches for her coat and stops, or when she actually says what's going on — the reader feels the weight of that. They've seen the pattern. They can measure the distance traveled.

Behavior as the Unit of Change

Character change shows in changed behavior — not in a character thinking about how much they've changed, and not in narration announcing it.

Announcing change

Over the months that followed, Cara gradually became more willing to trust people. She began to let her guard down.

Behavioral change

Six months ago, when the cab driver asked if she was okay — just the standard cheerful nothing of it — she would have said fine, thanks, looking out the window. Instead she said: "Not really. But I think I will be." The driver nodded, not surprised. She was a little surprised. Where had that come from.

The second version is a small moment. It doesn't announce transformation. It shows one instance of a behavior that would not have been possible before, and Cara notices it herself — which is its own form of showing without telling.

Using Callbacks to Show Change

One of the most effective techniques for showing character change is the callback — returning to a scene, object, line of dialogue, or behavior from earlier in the story, and showing how the character's relationship to it has shifted.

If a character struggles to say "I love you" in Act One, and says it easily in Act Three, the reader doesn't need to be told they've changed. The callback does the work.

If a character refuses to eat at a family dinner in an early scene — leaves food on their plate, gives clipped answers, leaves as soon as they can — and then, later, stays at the table after the meal and helps clear the plates, the reader feels the change without a word of explanation.

The callback works because the reader has already done the emotional work of the first scene. The second scene inherits that investment.

The Character Who Doesn't Change

Not all characters change, and that absence of change can be shown just as deliberately. A character who has every opportunity to learn and refuses is a tragedy. A character who learns nothing and suffers no consequences is a different story. Both require showing the same patterns repeating — behavior that could change and doesn't, choices made the same way despite mounting evidence.

Whatever the arc, the technique is the same: establish the behavior through scene, track it through the story, and let the ending — change or its absence — emerge from what the reader has observed rather than what the narration concludes.

Practice: Show the Before

Choose a character in your story who changes. Find or write the earliest scene in which their flaw or wound drives a decision. Write it so the behavior is fully visible — no narration explaining the character yet. Then write a later scene with the same type of choice. The change should be entirely in what they do, not in narration explaining that they've changed.

When Showing Goes Wrong

Showing is not automatically better than telling. Overdone, misdirected, or mechanically applied, showing creates its own set of problems. This chapter covers the four ways showing fails — and what to do about each one.

Over-Describing Mundane Action

> *The most common failure is showing every physical action when only the significant ones need showing. Beginning writers sometimes interpret "show don't tell" as "describe every movement."*

Over-shown

He reached for the door handle with his right hand, grasped the cold metal between his thumb and forefinger, twisted it counterclockwise, and pulled. The door swung open on its hinges. He stepped through, his left foot crossing the threshold first, and closed the door behind him, releasing the handle slowly so it wouldn't make noise.

Better

He opened the door and slipped inside.

The first version is showing in the technical sense — it's all action, no telling — but it shows the wrong things. Nobody reads a novel to experience a character opening a door. The physical mechanics of opening a door are not interesting. "He slipped inside" contains the one detail that matters: he was trying not to be heard.

The rule: show actions when the how of the action reveals something — character, emotion, stakes. Don't show the physical sequence when only the fact of the action matters.

Showing the Wrong Things

Showing requires editorial judgment. You can be technically excellent at showing and still produce a scene that doesn't work, because you're showing the wrong things for the scene you're writing.

If a character is rushing to deliver urgent news, a paragraph showing how they make their morning coffee is technically well-written showing — but it's the wrong thing to show. The reader feels the cost of every sentence between them and the urgent news.

Every scene has an emotional center — the one thing the scene is actually about. Showing should serve that center. Details that don't serve it slow the scene down and dilute its impact.

Before writing a scene, know its emotional center. What is this scene about, underneath the surface action? Show the details that make that center vivid, and tell — briefly — everything else.

Showing Without the Emotional Core

Some writers learn to show physical action extremely well but miss the emotional point entirely. The scene looks right and reads competently, but leaves the reader cold.

Weak showing

Tears ran down her cheeks and dropped onto her shirt. She pressed her lips together and looked at the ceiling. Her hands gripped the edge of the table.

Strong showing

She cried the way she did everything else — silently, so no one would worry about her.

The weak version shows tears, lip-pressing, and gripping. It's accurate physical description. But it tells us nothing about who this person is. The strong version is shorter and contains a single insight — the silence, the reason for it — that tells us everything we need to know about her character and makes the moment devastating.

Good showing combines external detail with interior revelation. The detail that sticks is always the one that tells the reader something true about who the character is.

Showing When Telling Would Serve Better

Showing slows narrative time. When you render an action in full sensory detail, you're expanding that moment, making the reader live through it. That's exactly right for a scene's emotional peak. It's exactly wrong for transitions, backstory, and the connective tissue between scenes.

A common over-showing pattern: dramatizing every conversation, every movement between locations, every routine action, rather than summarizing the ones that don't carry emotional weight.

Over-shown

She drove to the grocery store, found parking after three passes around the lot, walked through the automatic doors, got a cart, and spent forty minutes moving through the aisles, comparing prices and checking her list on her phone.

Better

She ran the usual errands. By the time she got home, it was almost four.

The second version tells, and it's exactly right. Nothing in that grocery trip matters to the story. Showing it would be fifty words of the reader's time and attention spent on nothing.

Showing everything equally is a way of showing nothing. The moments you expand with full showing should stand out because they're surrounded by efficient telling. Contrast is what gives showing its power.

Practice: Cut the Excess

Find a passage in your draft where you've shown more than necessary — described every physical movement, or lingered on a scene that doesn't carry emotional weight. Cut it to its single most important detail or action. Note what was lost and whether you miss it.

Purple Prose

Purple prose is writing so elaborate and ornamental that it pulls readers out of the story and makes them aware they're reading. It's not just overwriting — it's a specific failure mode where the language announces itself, where you feel the writer reaching for effect. The term comes from Horace, who compared ornate out-of-place passages to purple cloth sewn onto plain fabric — a patch that draws the eye for all the wrong reasons.

The crucial distinction: purple prose is not the same as vivid writing. Vivid writing uses precise, specific detail to put readers inside a scene. Purple prose uses decorative language to describe a scene from the outside, smothering it in adjectives and abstractions. The goal of vivid writing is transparency — the language disappears and the reader sees the scene. The goal of purple prose, consciously or not, is to impress.

Here is the same moment written three ways.

Flat (telling)

The sunset was beautiful.

Vivid (showing)

The sky went red over the rooftops, the light catching the dust in the air, and she stood watching until the streetlamps came on and she couldn't see the color anymore.

Purple

The magnificently resplendent crimson sunset cascaded brilliantly across the ethereally shimmering azure vault of heaven, nature's own masterpiece painted in hues of amber and rose, a transcendent spectacle that reduced all human suffering to blessed insignificance.

The flat version reports a fact. The vivid version puts the reader in the scene — a specific sky, a specific woman, a specific ending. The purple version buries both the sunset and the woman under the writer's vocabulary. Notice that the purple version actually contains less information. We know nothing about the woman, nothing specific about the light. We have adjectives instead of details.

Recognizing Purple Prose

The most reliable sign of purple prose is the stacking of adjectives and adverbs where one specific noun or verb would do the job better.

Purple

The tall, ancient, weather-beaten, moss-encrusted stone wall loomed forbiddingly before her.

Better

Moss had split the mortar in the old wall. She'd have to climb over it.

The second version is more specific and does more: the moss tells us age and climate, the split mortar tells us the wall is crumbling, and "she'd have to climb over it" puts us in the scene with stakes. Seven adjectives become one concrete detail and one action.

The second sign is abstract emotional language — words like anguish, torment, rapture, devastation — stacked on top of each other or attached to physical descriptions.

Purple

Tears of crystalline anguish cascaded down her alabaster cheeks like diamonds of sorrow upon virgin snow.

Better

Tears ran down her face. She didn't wipe them away.

The flat version tells. The purple version tells in elaborate dress. The better version shows — the detail of not wiping the tears does more emotional work than all the crystalline anguish in the world.

The third sign is the use of words chosen for their grandeur rather than their accuracy.

Purple

She masticated her sustenance contemplatively.

Better

She chewed slowly, staring at nothing.

"Masticated" is technically accurate but wrong — it draws attention to itself, makes the reader pause, yanks them out of the scene. "Chewed slowly, staring at nothing" is specific and invisible. The reader sees the woman; they don't see the writer reaching for the thesaurus.

The fourth sign is the overwrought metaphor — a comparison so strained or elaborate that it collapses under its own weight.

Purple

Her heart was a tempestuous ocean of roiling emotions, crashing endlessly against the jagged cliffs of her tortured soul, sending up great towers of spray that were her unshed tears.

Better

She had the feeling she recognized now — the one that came before she cried.

The purple version is three images competing to describe one thing. The better version is a single precise observation that tells you exactly where the character is emotionally and gives her interiority without naming the emotion.

The fifth sign — and one of the hardest to catch — is description that aestheticizes when it should ground.

Purple

Her luminous emerald orbs sparkled like precious gems beneath silken lashes.

Better

She had green eyes, the kind that changed in different light.

"Luminous emerald orbs" fails three ways: "orbs" is a word no one uses for eyes outside of purple prose; "luminous emerald" is a jewelry-catalog adjective stack; and "sparkled like precious gems" is a cliché dressed up in expensive language. The better version is specific, natural, and interesting without announcing itself.

The Spectrum: Too Flat, Just Right, Too Much

Writers often overcorrect. Told that their prose is purple, they strip it down to nothing and end up with writing that's equally problematic — flat, lifeless, clinical.

The target is neither extreme. Here is the same scene across the spectrum.

Flat

The old house was run-down. She went inside.

Vivid

The front step gave under her weight. Inside, the house smelled like her grandmother's closet — old wool and something sweeter, cedar or dried flowers — and she stood in the dark hallway listening to the silence the way you listen when you expect a sound.

Purple

She crossed the threshold of the venerable edifice, its timeworn magnificence whispering of bygone eras, the musty perfume of antiquity enveloping her like a tender embrace from the ghostly denizens of its storied past.

The flat version reports. The purple version decorates. The vivid version puts the reader in the house — specific smell, specific sensation underfoot, specific quality of attention. It uses comparison (like her grandmother's closet, like you listen when you expect a sound) to give the scene emotional texture without announcing it.

The test for whether your writing is vivid or purple: does the language make the scene more real, or does it make the language more visible? If you read a sentence and think "that's beautifully written," you may have a problem. You should be too busy being in the scene to notice the sentences.

Fixing Purple Prose

Step one: find the purple passage and identify what it's actually trying to do. Is it describing a setting? Conveying an emotion?

Showing a character noticing something? Once you know the purpose, ask: what specific detail would achieve that purpose?

Before (purple emotion)

Overwhelming waves of devastating grief crashed through the very depths of her tormented soul, leaving nothing but the ashen ruins of her former joy.

After (vivid emotion)

She sat at the kitchen table for a long time after she heard. The refrigerator hummed. Outside, a neighbor was mowing his lawn, and she thought distantly: it's too early in the season for that.

The after version uses externals — mundane, ordinary, slightly wrong details — to show the shock and dissociation of acute grief. It doesn't name grief once.

Step two: cut every adjective that isn't doing specific work. If you can remove an adjective and the noun still means the same thing, cut it. "Old wall" tells you something. "Ancient, crumbling, moss-encrusted, foreboding wall" tells you the same thing four times plus one editorial conclusion you should let the reader draw.

Step three: replace abstract nouns with concrete ones. "Sadness" becomes the coffee she doesn't finish. "Fear" becomes the door she checks twice. "Joy" becomes the thing she almost says and doesn't.

Step four: read it aloud. Purple prose sounds embarrassing when spoken. If you can't read a sentence to another person without feeling like you're performing, the sentence is performing — and readers will feel it.

When Ornate Writing Works

Not all elaborate language is purple prose. Some genres — Gothic horror, certain literary fiction, historical romance set in periods with a grander register — can sustain a richer, more formal prose style. The difference is always the same: does the language serve the story, or is it serving itself?

Gothic horror can use elaborate language to create dread and atmosphere, as long as the language is precise rather than decorative. "The house had a face" is Gothic and vivid. "The magnificent and terrifying edifice loomed with palpable menace" is Gothic and purple.

Historical fiction set in periods with formal speech patterns can use a more elevated register, as long as it matches the character's voice and education. A Victorian gentleman's letters would sound different from a farmhand's thoughts. But within each voice, precision still beats decoration.

The test is always: is this language serving the reader's experience of the scene, or is it serving the writer's desire to sound a certain way? Readers forgive a great deal when they're inside a story. They disengage the moment they're made to admire the curtains.

Your job is not to write beautifully. Your job is to write so that readers forget they're reading.

Practice: Find Your Purple

Read the last three pages of your draft and mark every adjective and adverb. For each one: is this the most specific word, or is it decoration? For each adjective, ask whether the noun carries the weight alone. For each adverb, ask whether a stronger verb makes it redundant. Cut or replace the five weakest.

Genre Applications: Show Don't Tell Across Fiction Types

The principles in this book apply to every genre of fiction. But how you apply them — which techniques matter most, where the traps are, what your readers most need to experience — varies significantly depending on what you're writing. This chapter shows how show-don't-tell operates in five major genres.

Thriller and Mystery

In thrillers and mysteries, everything the reader notices has to feel like potential evidence. Your job is to show enough that the reader is building theories, but not so much that the answer is obvious. Every detail the detective or protagonist notices either is a clue or feels like one.

The most common mistake in this genre is telling the reader what's suspicious rather than showing behavior that is suspicious.

Telling

Something seemed off about the man at the end of the bar.

Showing

The man at the end of the bar was drinking soda water with a lime. He'd had three of them in the last hour and hadn't looked at his phone once. He was watching the door in the mirror above the shelf.

The second version lets the reader feel what the protagonist feels — the accumulation of small, specific wrong notes. In mystery fiction, this accumulation is the entire mechanism. The reader is playing the game. Give them the pieces.

Pacing is also critical in thrillers. This is a genre that earns its telling. In a chase scene or a ticking-clock sequence, short declarative telling sentences are often more effective than detailed showing:

She ran. Three floors to the exit. Two.

In action sequences, telling accelerates urgency. Use it.

Thriller: Showing and Pace

Thrillers operate on a faster showing/telling ratio than most other genres, and knowing when to shift between them is the essential skill. The rule of thumb: show what creates dread, tell what gets characters from one dread to the next.

Slow-burn tension requires sustained showing — the accumulation of wrong details, the held breath, the thing that doesn't quite fit. The soda water man at the bar. The shadow that doesn't move. These need full presence on the page because the reader needs to feel the building unease, not be told it exists.

But when the action breaks — when the chase starts, the gun appears, the clock starts ticking — the telling takes over. Short, declarative sentences. No time for sensory texture. The prose itself becomes urgent.

Slow-burn (showing)

> *The elevator doors had been opening and closing on the fourth floor for twelve minutes. She'd watched the number flicker each time. No one got out. No one got in.*

Action (telling)

> *She ran. Four flights. The stairwell door hit the wall behind her. She didn't look back.*

The contrast between these modes is itself a tool. When fast prose slows down — when you bring showing back into a chase — readers feel the deceleration as heightened danger, not as relief. A character noticing one specific detail during flight (the smell of cigarette smoke, a child's bike in the corridor) signals that this moment is more significant than the running.

Internal panic in a thriller is different from interior life in literary fiction. It should be shorter, more fragmented, cut off mid-thought by external events. The character doesn't have the luxury of a complete internal experience. Show that truncation.

Too much interior in a thriller

> *She ran, her heart hammering, thinking about how she had never really believed this kind of thing could happen to her, remembering all the times she'd walked this route alone and felt perfectly safe.*

Fractured interior — more effective

> *She ran. The thought arrived: I parked on three. The thought disappeared. She ran.*

Romance

Romance lives and dies on emotional interiority and sensory detail. Readers of romance want to be inside the experience — the specific texture of attraction, the exact quality of longing, the first moment of physical contact. Summarizing these experiences is one of the fastest ways to lose a romance reader.

The trap unique to romance is telling the emotional conclusion without showing the moment that creates it.

Telling

She realized she was falling for him.

Showing

> He reached across her to open the car door — unnecessary, she had her keys — and she noticed the smell of him, warm cotton and something faintly sharp, and when he stepped back his arm brushed hers and she said thank you and got into the car and sat there for a long moment before starting the engine.

Romance showing is intimate, specific, and body-focused. It's what a person actually notices when they're becoming attracted to someone: the exact smell, the specific texture of a voice, the way someone occupies space. Generic showing — "his strong hands," "her beautiful laugh" — fails romance because it doesn't create the particularity of desire. Specificity is what makes attraction feel real.

Romance: The Arc of Falling in Love

Romance has a challenge no other genre shares: the emotional arc of falling in love needs to be shown across an entire book, not just in a single scene. Attraction in Chapter Two cannot feel identical to love in Chapter Twenty-Two. The showing has to escalate.

The stages of falling in love each have a distinct physical texture. Early attraction is involuntary, fragmented, often surprising — the character notices things without meaning to. Middle-stage feeling is more searching, more anxious; the character is trying to read the other person, looking for evidence. Deep love is specific in a way early attraction isn't — it's built from accumulated particular knowledge.

Early attraction

> *He laughed at something across the room — she didn't see what — and she noticed, filed it away without knowing she was filing.*

Growing investment

> *She caught herself rehearsing what she'd say to him. Not planning — just running it, the way you run a song in your head without meaning to start.*

The middle stage — growing investment — is where many romance writers stall, because it's the hardest to show. Early attraction is involuntary; deep love is accumulated. But the middle is active and anxious: the character is trying to read another person, looking for evidence, managing their own hope. They are both doing it and trying not to be seen doing it.

The key is showing the surveillance and the self-monitoring simultaneously.

Growing investment (fuller)

> *She told herself she wasn't watching for him. Then when he came in twenty minutes late she realized she'd registered the twenty minutes. She went back to her notes. He sat two rows ahead and one seat left, which she now knew was exactly far enough that she could watch him without it being obvious if he turned around.*

That's the middle stage: not just noticing, but catching yourself noticing, and continuing anyway. The self-awareness that doesn't stop the behavior is what makes this stage specific.

The hardest moment to show in stage two is the misread signal — when a character interprets ambiguous behavior as confirmation of what they want to believe. This is where stage two gets its specific anxious quality. The character isn't just watching; they're building a case, and the evidence keeps being inconclusive.

Misread signal

> *He held the door open, which didn't mean anything. Everyone held doors open. She went through and said thank you and he said you're welcome, and she spent the next twenty minutes deciding whether he'd said it the way you say it to anyone, or differently.*

That's the texture of stage two: behavior that could mean something or nothing, and a character who can't stop trying to read it. The showing stays in the character's interpretation — the gap between what actually happened (he held a door) and the significance she's involuntarily assigned to it.

Complicated or resisted attraction follows the same logic but adds conflict: the character wants to stop noticing and can't. The surveillance becomes evidence against themselves.

Resisted attraction

> *He said something kind to the person next to him — she didn't catch what — and she thought: don't. Just don't. She went back to her phone. Found herself reading the same sentence four times. He laughed, low, at something she hadn't heard, and she pressed her thumbnail into her palm and kept her eyes on the screen.*

Deep feeling

> *She knew the sound his keys made coming out of his pocket. She knew he held his breath when he was reading something he didn't want to be moved by. She knew these things the way you*

know the layout of your own apartment — not thought about, just known.

The progression from involuntary noticing to specific accumulated knowledge is the arc of love made visible. Each stage requires different showing.

The black moment — the low point where the relationship fractures — requires the same precision. Don't name devastation. Show what breaks through the numbness. The character who has learned to love someone specifically has specific things to mourn.

Telling

She was heartbroken.

Showing

She kept nearly texting him things. A dog on the street that was exactly the kind of dog he'd stop to talk to. A menu item he'd have made a face at. She'd open her phone and there'd be nowhere to send it.

Science Fiction and Fantasy

World-building is the central challenge of speculative fiction, and it's where show-don't-tell is most difficult to apply. The temptation is to explain the world before putting readers in it. The better approach is to drop readers into a fully realized world and let them assemble understanding from what they observe.

Telling

In the world of Arethia, magic came from the user's memories. The more significant the memory, the stronger the spell.

Showing

> Soren didn't reach for a weapon. He reached for his dead brother's face — the specific weight of that afternoon, the smell of rain on stone, the way his brother had laughed right before he fell. The air thickened. The wall behind him cracked.

The second version teaches the magic system through character action and consequence. The reader learns by observing. This is more immersive and far more memorable than explanation, because the reader has to do the small cognitive work of figuring it out.

The same principle applies to technology, societies, and alien species. Show behavior. Show consequences. Let the reader infer the rules. Explanation is always the last resort.

Literary Fiction

Literary fiction tends to use a higher density of interiority than other genres, and it's the genre where free indirect discourse — thought embedded seamlessly in prose — is most central. Literary readers expect to live inside a consciousness, not just observe from outside it.

The specific trap for literary fiction is beautiful description that observes without feeling. You can write a gorgeous paragraph about a landscape that tells the reader nothing about the character experiencing it. In literary fiction, everything observed should reveal the observer.

Telling

The sunset was extraordinary.

Showing (literary)

The sunset was doing its usual work — reds, the whole performance — and she sat on the hood of the car watching it and thought that she would have called her mother to describe it, and then remembered she couldn't do that anymore.

The landscape is almost irrelevant. What matters is what the character does with it. In literary fiction, the world exists as a function of the character's interior life. Show the world; show what the world means to this particular person.

Young Adult

YA fiction often involves protagonists experiencing intense emotions for the first time, which means the emotional stakes of any given scene are extremely high. The worst thing a YA author can do is summarize those emotions from the outside.

YA readers are reading to feel. They want to feel falling in love, being humiliated, having a parent disappoint them, finding a best friend. They need to live those experiences through the character, not read a report of them.

The technical challenge of YA is that your protagonist is often in overwhelming emotional territory but may lack the vocabulary or self-awareness to name what they're feeling. This is a showing opportunity, not a limitation. An overwhelmed teenager doesn't think "I felt profound social anxiety." They think about how the lunch tray is too heavy and they don't know where to sit and their face is hot and everyone is going to look at them.

Telling

Starting at a new school was the worst experience of her life.

Showing

> She stood at the entrance to the cafeteria holding her tray and the noise hit her like something physical. Six hundred people. She didn't know one of them. She looked for somewhere that wasn't full, wasn't too empty, wasn't too close to where anyone interesting might sit. The tray was heavier than it should have been. She walked toward the back.

Every genre has its own rhythm, its own reader expectations, and its own pressure points. But the underlying principle holds across all of them: trust your reader to experience the story you're creating. Show them what your character experiences. Let them draw conclusions. They'll draw better ones than you could tell them.

Practice: Apply the Genre Rule

Take one scene from your work-in-progress. Identify your genre. Apply the specific trap from this chapter: in thriller, are you over-explaining suspense? In romance, are you naming attraction instead of showing it? In literary fiction, are your descriptions observing without revealing the observer? Rewrite two sentences using the genre-specific technique.

Practice: Run the First Two Passes

Take one page of your draft. Run the emotion word hunt: circle every word that names a feeling (angry, sad, afraid, excited). Then run the filter word hunt: circle every filter word (noticed, realized, felt, seemed, heard). Count the circles. Rewrite the three highest-priority instances — the ones where showing would make the biggest difference.

Finding and Fixing Telling in Your Draft

Reading about showing is one thing. Opening your own manuscript and knowing what to look for — and what to do when you find it — is something else. This chapter is a practical guide to the revision pass.

The good news: telling leaves tracks. Once you know what to look for, you can find it systematically.

Pass One: The Emotion Word Hunt

Go through your manuscript searching for direct emotion words: angry, sad, happy, afraid, excited, nervous, relieved, ashamed, proud, confused, devastated, joyful, depressed, frustrated, and any other word that names a feeling state rather than describes behavior.

Every instance is a candidate for revision. Not all of them will need rewriting — sometimes a brief emotion label is the right tool. But each one should be a conscious choice, not a default.

When you find one, ask: what would this character do, say, or notice that would let the reader feel this emotion rather than be told it? Then write that instead.

Telling

He was furious when he read the letter.

Revision question: what does furious look like for this specific character in this specific moment?

Showing

He read the letter twice. Then he folded it along its original creases, very carefully, and set it on the counter. He went to the window. Outside, someone was raking leaves. He watched them for a long time.

The behavior is specific to this character — the careful folding, the displacement activity, the long blank stare. That specificity is what makes it showing rather than a general description of anger.

Finding the telling is the easier half. The harder half is knowing what to write instead. Identifying a filter word or an emotion label tells you what to cut — it doesn't automatically tell you what the replacement looks like. If you find yourself staring at a sentence after removing 'she felt afraid' and not knowing how to show it, that's not a failure. It means you need to go deeper into the character's specific physical experience. The Strong Verbs chapter and the Interiority chapter both give you tools for this: a strong verb shows the action; the body's interior senses show the state. The revision pass finds the problems. The showing techniques you've practiced give you the solutions.

Pass Two: The Filter Word Hunt

Search for filter words — verbs that put a layer between the reader and the experience: saw, heard, noticed, felt, realized, understood, wondered, thought, knew, seemed, appeared.

Telling (filtered)

She noticed that the room had gone quiet.

Showing (direct)

The room had gone quiet.

Telling (filtered)

He realized he had made a mistake.

Showing (direct)

The wrong name was already out of his mouth.

Filter words aren't always wrong. In scenes where the act of perceiving is itself important — where a character is struggling to understand something, or where their delayed realization is the point — filter words can carry weight. But when they're just habit, removing them puts the reader directly inside the moment.

Pass Three: The "Was" and "Were" Audit

Sentences built around was and were are often static — they describe a state rather than an action. Static sentences stack up to produce flat passages.

Search your manuscript for was and were, then ask: can this be rewritten as action?

Static

The market was crowded and noisy. There were vendors on both sides of the street.

Active

Vendors lined both sides of the street, shouting prices over each other, and the crowd moved in the way crowds do — with its own momentum, carrying you whether you wanted to go or not.

The active version is showing because it puts the reader inside the experience of the crowded market rather than reporting its properties.

Pass Four: The Adverb Check

Adverbs modifying dialogue tags and action verbs are almost always telling. They announce an emotion or quality that the writing itself should be demonstrating.

Telling (adverb doing the work)

"I don't care," she said coldly.

"Get out," he said angrily.

She walked quickly to the door.

Revision question: what action, detail, or dialogue would show this without the adverb?

Showing

"I don't care." She turned back to her book.

He didn't say it again. He just looked at the door.

She was at the door before she'd decided to go.

For each adverb, find the specific behavior it's covering for and write that behavior instead.

Pass Five: The Dialogue Tag Check

Read through your dialogue tags — said, asked, replied — and look for expressive tags: shouted, whispered, snapped, pleaded, growled, sighed. Each one is doing a job that an action beat would do better.

Not every expressive tag needs rewriting. Whispered and shouted convey volume, which matters. But snapped, growled, pleaded, and sighed are almost always telling the reader how a line of dialogue sounds rather than letting the dialogue sound that way.

When you find them, try replacing with said plus an action beat and see if the result is stronger.

The Order of the Passes

Do these passes separately. Looking for everything at once is overwhelming and you'll miss things. One pass for emotion words. One pass for filter words. One pass for was/were. Adverbs and dialogue tags can be combined since they're both about showing vs. announcing.

After each pass, read the revised section aloud. Purple prose sounds ridiculous out loud. Flat telling sounds inert. Strong showing reads the way good conversation sounds — like something is actually happening.

You won't catch everything. Nobody does on one pass. But these five sweeps will transform a first draft's telling into the kind of specific, scene-level showing that puts readers inside your story.

Practice: The Full Revision

Take two pages of your draft and run all five passes in sequence: emotion words, filter words, was/were, adverbs, dialogue tags. Don't try to fix everything — identify the single most important change in each pass. Make those five changes and read the revised pages aloud.

Using This Book to Give Feedback

The vocabulary in this book — filter words, emotion labels, explaining the image, purple prose — is also the vocabulary of useful feedback. When you're reading another writer's work, whether in a critique group, a workshop, or an informal exchange, the same framework applies.

The most useful feedback names the type of issue specifically rather than describing the feeling it produces. "This felt distant" is accurate but not actionable. "This paragraph has three filter words in a row — noticed, felt, seemed — and they're pushing the reader outside the character's experience" tells the writer exactly what to look for and fix.

Here are the most common issues and how to name them in a critique:

Instead of: "I didn't feel connected to the character"

> *Try: "The emotion is being named rather than shown — she felt devastated, he was furious. What would each of them do or notice that would let the reader feel it?"*

Instead of: "This scene felt slow"

> *Try: "The scene is showing actions that don't carry emotional weight — every physical movement is described. What is the one thing that matters here? Tell the rest."*

Instead of: "I didn't believe this character"

> *Try: "The character is being described by adjective — he was generous, she was stubborn. Show me one scene where the behavior produces that conclusion."*

Instead of: "This is too much telling"

> *Try: "This paragraph has filter words that create distance — she realized, he noticed, it seemed. Remove them and put the reader directly at the observation."*

The goal of specific feedback is to give the writer a procedure, not a verdict. “I didn’t feel it” is a verdict. “Here’s what to look for and how to change it” is a procedure. Procedures produce better revisions.

Appendix B: An Annotated Scene

This appendix shows scenes from five genres, each in three stages: a first draft with telling problems marked, comments explaining each mark, and the revised version after changes. Read the draft first, then the comments, then the revision. Reading all five genres will show you how the same principles apply differently depending on what you’re writing.

Literary Fiction

The draft below shows the most common literary fiction telling problems: opening with backstory, filter words, emotion labels, and explaining images that should speak for themselves.

The Draft

It had been three weeks since her mother’s funeral. [1] Nora felt like she wasn’t ready, [2] but she forced herself to drive to her parents’ house to sort through things anyway.

Her brother had offered to help, but she had told him no. She felt guilty about that. [3] She arrived feeling irritated and confused about her own emotions. [4]

She put her key in the lock. She was surprised that it still worked. [5] She went inside.

Inside, the house smelled like her mother, which made her feel sad and overwhelmed. [6] It was hard to be there.

She walked down the hallway. She felt like she wanted to go to the kitchen [7] because that was where her mother had always spent most of her time.

The dishes in the sink had been washed and put away. Someone had clearly come in and cleaned up after the funeral. [8]

On the counter she noticed [9] a notepad that had her mother's handwriting on it. It was a grocery list with items like milk and bread on it. [10] It made her feel emotional, [11] so she put the notepad in her pocket.

She ended up staying for about two hours, but she was unable to bring herself to actually sort through anything. She left feeling like she had failed at the task she came to do. [12]

Comments

1 **TELLING — opens with backstory instead of scene —** Starting with a time stamp before the scene begins. Open with her arriving, and let the time elapsed arrive in a brief transition sentence that stays in motion.

2 **FILTER WORD + EMOTION LABEL** — 'Felt like she wasn't ready' names the feeling and distances us with a filter. Cut both. Show what not-ready looks like in her body or behavior when she arrives.

3 **EMOTION LABEL** — 'Felt guilty' announces the feeling. Replace with the specific thought or behavior that carries it — the thing she replays, the thing she can't stop hearing.

4 **DOUBLE TELLING** — 'Feeling irritated and confused about her own emotions' — two emotion labels and a meta-commentary. Nothing shown. Replace with displaced behavior: angry at the wrong things, at herself, at the drive.

5 **FILTER WORD + WAS CONSTRUCTION** — 'She was surprised' names the state. Rewrite so the surprise is in the observation itself: the key working feels wrong, like the house should have known.

6 **EMOTION LABEL UNDOING SENSORY WORK** — The smell was doing its job. 'Which made her feel sad and overwhelmed' explains what the smell already communicated. Cut everything after the comma.

7 **FILTER WORD** — 'She felt like she wanted to go' — three filter words before the action. She just goes. Let the destination explain itself.

8 **EXPLAINING THE IMAGE** — 'Someone had clearly come in and cleaned up after the funeral' tells the reader what the clean dishes already imply. Trust the image.

9 **FILTER WORD** — 'She noticed' creates distance. Remove it. Put the reader directly at the object.

10 **DILUTED DETAIL** — 'Items like milk and bread' — 'items like' weakens the specificity. Name the items as their own sentence: Milk. Bread.

11 **EMPTY EMOTION LABEL** — 'It made her feel emotional' — the emptiest possible statement. Replace with what she does.

12 **EXPLAINING THE ENDING** — The last sentence tells us how to read the scene. Cut it. 'She stayed for two hours. She didn't sort anything.' is the ending.

After Revision

Three weeks after the funeral, Nora went back to her parents' house to start sorting through things.

Her brother had offered to come. She'd said no, and then felt guilty about it the whole drive over, which meant she arrived irritated at herself and not sure who to blame.

The key still worked, which surprised her, as if she'd expected the house to have changed the locks.

Inside smelled the same. That was the worst part.

She stood in the hallway for a moment, then went to the kitchen, because that's where her mother had always been.

The dishes were done. She didn't know who had done them.

She found a notepad on the counter with her mother's handwriting. A grocery list. Milk. Bread. The ordinary things. She put it in her pocket and didn't know why.

She stayed for two hours. She didn't sort anything.

The revised scene is shorter. No emotion is named except in passing ('felt guilty' is kept because its presence in a subordinate clause, immediately overridden by displaced behavior, is realistic). Every other feeling arrives through action, detail, and what the character does with what she finds.

Thriller

The draft below contains the most common thriller telling problems: named fear, explained suspense, filter words that soften impact, and interior monologue that slows the pace when it should be accelerating.

The Draft

Detective Reyes felt nervous [1] as she approached the warehouse. It was late, and the building seemed threatening and dark. [2] She noticed [3] that there were no lights on in the windows.

She felt like she should call for backup, [4] but she was worried that he might hear her if she used the radio. [5] She hesitated for a moment, thinking about whether it was safe. [6]

Then she heard a sound from inside. It was a scraping noise, and it made her afraid. [7] She realized [8] he was still in there.

She took a deep breath to calm herself down. [9] Then she pushed open the door and went inside.

Comments

1 **EMOTION LABEL** — 'Felt nervous' tells us her state. In a thriller, naming nervous diffuses tension rather than building it. Replace with the physical signs of her body under stress.

2 **DOUBLE ADJECTIVE TELLING** — 'Seemed threatening and dark' — both are conclusions. Show the building. Let the reader feel threatened.

3 **FILTER WORD** — 'She noticed that' places the reader one step back. Remove it. Put the observation directly on the page.

4 **FILTER WORD + EMOTION LABEL** — 'Felt like she should' and 'was worried' both tell her state. In a thriller, deliberation needs to be kinetic. Show the calculation — hand on radio, hand stopping — not the feeling that prompts it.

5 **EXPLANATION AFTER INSTINCT** — 'She was worried that he might hear her' explains her decision instead of letting the decision explain itself. The withheld radio call is already telling. Don't explain it.

6 **TELLING THE THINKING** — 'Thinking about whether it was safe' — a character in danger doesn't have this kind of reflective pause. Interiority here should be fractured, not summarized.

7 **EMOTION LABEL AT THE PIVOT** — 'It made her afraid' — the scene's hinge gets the emptiest possible response. Replace with her body's reaction.

8 **FILTER WORD** — 'She realized' distances the reader. Cut it. The fact is: he was still in there. Land on it with her.

9 **EXPLAINING THE ACTION'S PURPOSE** — 'To calm herself down' tells us why. The breath itself carries that without commentary.

After Revision

Reyes cut the engine half a block out and walked the rest. The warehouse sat dark — every window dark, no sound, the loading dock door hanging two inches open when it should have been chained.

Her hand found the radio. Stopped. He'd hear the squelch.

Inside: a scrape. Metal on concrete.

Still there.

She pushed the door open with her shoulder and went in.

The revised version is less than half the length. No emotion labels, no filter words, no explained decisions. Reyes's fear is in her behavior — cutting the engine early, stopping her hand on the radio. The realization is a fragment: 'Still there.' The pace never stops.

Romance

Romance telling problems are specific: naming attraction instead of showing it, explaining what physical details mean, and summarizing emotional moments that need to be lived through.

The Draft

Maya felt attracted to him from the moment she saw him. [1] He was handsome and confident, [2] and there was something about his smile that she really liked. [3]

When he came over to talk to her, she felt nervous and excited. [4] She tried to act normal even though she was very aware of how close he was standing to her. [5]

"I've been wanting to meet you," he said. His voice was nice. [6] Maya felt her heart rate increase. [7] She realized [8] she was falling for him.

It was clear that there was chemistry between them. [9] She hoped he felt the same way. [10]

Comments

1 **NAMING ATTRACTION** — 'Felt attracted to him' announces the conclusion the scene should be building toward. Start with what she notices, not what she feels.

2 **ADJECTIVE LABELS** — 'Handsome and confident' are labels. Every reader imagines these differently. Replace with

the specific physical detail that makes this particular man register.

3 **VAGUE NOTICING** — 'Something about his smile' – 'something about' is a writer avoiding specificity. What specifically? The detail carries the attraction.

4 **DOUBLE EMOTION LABEL** — 'Nervous and excited' – named together they flatten each other. Each produces different physical signatures. Pick one and show it in the body.

5 **TELLING THE AWARENESS** — 'Very aware of how close he was standing' — told from outside. Show what awareness at close proximity actually feels like: what she stops noticing, what her body does.

6 **WEAK DETAIL** — 'His voice was nice' – nice is the emptiest adjective in English. This is the first time she hears him speak. It deserves specificity.

7 **CLINICAL PHYSIOLOGY** — 'Heart rate increase' is distancing. The physical experience of attraction is more specific and stranger than an elevated pulse.

8 **FILTER WORD + PREMATURE CONCLUSION** — 'She realized she was falling for him' — filter word, and naming the arc before it's been built. This is a first conversation. Don't tell the reader; let them start to suspect.

9 **STATING THE SUBTEXT** — 'It was clear that there was chemistry' — if it's clear, it doesn't need to be said. Trust the scene you just wrote.

10 **TELLING THE HOPE** — 'She hoped he felt the same way' – summary instead of moment. End in a specific image, not a statement of her emotional state.

After Revision

The thing she noticed first was that he laughed at something across the room — she didn't see what — and then caught himself, like he'd made a noise louder than he'd intended.

When he came over she lost three or four words of what her friend was saying. Not because he'd done anything. She'd just stopped processing.

"I've been wanting to meet you." Low. Like he meant it specifically.

Maya looked down at her drink. When she looked back up he was still watching her. She said something — she'd reconstruct later what it was — and he smiled in a way that suggested she'd said the right thing.

She stayed at the party another hour. She was aware, the entire time, of exactly where he was in the room.

No emotion is named. Attraction is entirely in behavior: the involuntary attention, the lost words, the room-tracking. The reader builds the feeling from evidence — which means they feel it.

Science Fiction and Fantasy

Speculative fiction telling problems cluster around world-building: explaining rules instead of showing them in action, announcing stakes, and over-narrating the unfamiliar.

The Draft

The colony ship had been traveling for two hundred years. [1] Commander Vasquez felt the weight of responsibility for the eight thousand people in cryo-sleep on her shoulders. [2]

The ship's AI, called ARIA, was very intelligent and helpful. [3] It could calculate trajectories and also understood human emotions. [4]

"We have a problem," ARIA said in a calm voice that seemed designed to not alarm anyone. [5] Vasquez felt worried. [6]

"The third cryo-chamber has malfunctioned," ARIA explained. [7] This was very bad because the people inside would die if it wasn't fixed. [8] Vasquez realized [9] she would have to make a difficult decision.

Comments

1 **INFO DUMP AS OPENER** — Opening with a two-hundred-year backstory fact before the scene begins. Start in the moment. Let the two hundred years arrive through context and habit.

2 **TELLING THE STAKES + EMOTION LABEL** — 'Felt the weight of responsibility' names both emotion and stakes in one generic phrase. Show her relationship to those eight thousand lives — what she does with it, how it lives in her daily behavior.

3 **ADJECTIVE CHARACTERIZATION** — 'Very intelligent and helpful' — two adjectives that tell us nothing specific. Show ARIA being intelligent. Let helpfulness emerge from behavior.

4 **CAPABILITY LIST** — 'Could calculate trajectories and also understood human emotions' — a list is not characterization. Show ARIA doing one of these things in a way that reveals its specific character.

5 **EXPLAINING THE TONE** — 'In a calm voice that seemed designed to not alarm anyone' — the reader should feel the

calibrated calm, not be told it's calibrated. Cut the explanation.

6 **EMOTION LABEL AT PIVOT POINT** — The scene's critical turn gets 'felt worried.' A commander responsible for eight thousand lives has a more specific relationship to bad news.

7 **EXPRESSIVE DIALOGUE TAG** — 'ARIA explained' — the line is already explanatory. Use 'said' or no tag.

8 **EXPLAINING THE STAKES** — 'This was very bad because the people inside would die' tells the reader what they can already evaluate. Trust them to understand what a malfunctioning cryo-chamber means.

9 **FILTER WORD + VAGUE CONSEQUENCE** — 'Realized she would have to make a difficult decision' — filter word and naming the decision type rather than its weight. End in the decision's arrival.

After Revision

Two hundred years out, and Vasquez still did her rounds at 0300 the way she had done at 0300 on day one. Eight thousand people down in the dark. She had learned not to think of them as people exactly — it made the math impossible — but she had never entirely stopped.

"Commander." ARIA's voice had a register it used when it was managing her. She'd mapped it over the years: fractionally lower, fractionally slower. She hated that she found it comforting.

"Cryo-chamber three."

Vasquez was already moving. The corridor lights came up as she walked. "How many?"

"Four hundred and twelve."

She didn't stop walking. There was nothing to do with that number yet except carry it.

World-building arrives through action and habit — the 0300 rounds, the two hundred years, the eight thousand. ARIA's character is shown through its calibrated voice and Vasquez's awareness of it. The stakes land through her response: not grief — just the decision to keep moving.

Young Adult

YA telling problems are often about over-explaining the emotional experience of adolescence — naming feelings the character may not have words for, and explaining social situations that should be shown through behavior.

The Draft

It was Priya's first day at Jefferson High and she felt extremely anxious and out of place. [1] Everyone seemed to know each other already, which made her feel like an outsider. [2]

She walked into the cafeteria and immediately felt overwhelmed by the noise and the number of people. [3] She didn't know where to sit and felt embarrassed about that. [4]

A girl named Jade, who was clearly popular and confident, [5] noticed Priya standing there looking lost. [6]

"You can sit with us if you want," Jade said in a friendly way. [7] Priya felt surprised and grateful. [8] She felt like maybe things would be okay after all. [9]

Comments

1 **DOUBLE EMOTION LABEL AT OPENING** — Starting with 'felt extremely anxious and out of place' names both feelings before the scene can create them. Put the reader inside the anxiety — body, sensation, specific wrongness — don't announce it.

2 **TOLD SOCIAL OBSERVATION + NAMED FEELING** — 'Everyone seemed to know each other' is a told summary. Show it in specific details: who's laughing with who, what she can't read, what she misses. 'Feel like an outsider' names the conclusion instead of building it.

3 **EMOTION LABEL FOR PHYSICAL EXPERIENCE** — 'Felt overwhelmed by the noise' — the noise is the scene. The overwhelm should be in Priya's sensory experience, not in the word 'overwhelmed.'

4 **DOUBLE TELLING** — 'Didn't know where to sit' is fine — it's behavior. 'Felt embarrassed about that' explains the behavior's meaning. Cut it. The not-knowing is already embarrassing.

5 **ADJECTIVE CHARACTER LABELS** — 'Clearly popular and confident' — both conclusions. Show Jade in a way that makes the reader draw those conclusions.

6 **FILTER WORD + TELLING THE VISIBLE** — 'Noticed Priya standing there looking lost' — filter word, and telling us what Priya looks like rather than showing her through Jade's action.

7 **EXPLAINING THE TONE** — 'In a friendly way' — the invitation already carries this. Cut the tag.

8 **DOUBLE EMOTION LABEL** — Two named feelings in response to one moment. Show the physical experience of the surprise instead.

9 **SUMMARIZING THE TURN** — 'Felt like maybe things would be okay after all' — the scene's payoff told as summary. End in a moment.

After Revision

The cafeteria hit her before she was through the door: five hundred conversations at once, trays clattering, sneakers on linoleum, and underneath it all that specific school smell, industrial cleaner and something that was supposed to be pizza.

She stood at the edge with her tray. There were tables everywhere and she couldn't read any of them — who sat where, whether the empty seats were empty-available or empty-for-a-reason. Back home she'd have known without thinking.

A girl at the nearest table looked up. Not unfriendly. Just looked.

"You can sit here," she said. Not 'if you want.' Just: you can sit here.

Priya sat down. Her tray made a sound on the table. The girl went back to her phone. Priya unfolded her napkin and for the first time all day her shoulders came down from where they'd been, somewhere near her ears.

The anxiety is entirely physical — the sensory assault, the unreadable tables, the shoulders near her ears. The social dynamic is in the word choice: 'you can sit here,' not 'if you want.' The relief is in the body. Nothing is named.

Appendix: Research Resources for Writers

Describing how something appears to an observer can be difficult, especially when writing settings or situations outside your direct experience. If you've never been to a haunted house, how do you describe one? How do you tell your readers what it looks like to go into the bedroom of a 100-year-old home that hasn't been occupied by living beings for decades?

For a crime drama, how do you describe a crack house? The inside of the forensics lab? The tests that the various specialists use? The appearance of a police officer as he's chasing a suspect?

If your story involves a character inside of a Catholic Church, and you've never been inside one, how do you describe it in a believable way?

If you've never seen, held or fired a gun, how does a writer show the weight of the gun, the recoil, the smoke, and so forth?

It can be difficult to show something you haven't experienced. How does a writer get around that?

The answer: use the tools at hand. If you have access to the Internet, you have plenty of ways to get a visual image of anything that you can think of. There are probably hundreds of billions of images and videos stored all over the web, and all you must do is search for them.

Unfortunately, a picture doesn't tell you how something smells, how heavy it is, or the emotions it evokes.

However, there are countless ways to experience objects and environments so you can write them convincingly.

I've included some suggestions about how you can improve your writing with experiences. This is not an all-inclusive list–I am sure you can think of many other ways to learn about situations, scenery, emotions and so forth.

Museums

When I lived in Los Angeles I regularly visited the Los Angeles Museum of Natural History. This remarkable building contains hundreds of thousands of objects in display cases, open seven days a week for a small entrance fee.

Like many museums, this one contains a special room for the schools in the area housing tens of thousands of objects that can be handled, touched, picked up, dropped, thrown, and smelled to your heart's content.

As you enter the room, there is a large stuffed polar bear right out in the open that you can touch. In the cabinets around the room are boxes containing different objects such as rocks, wood, fur, and just about anything else you can think of.

Other rooms contain dinosaurs or at least their bones. This is great if you need to get a feel for how big the dinosaur is in comparison to a human being.

Museums are an underused resource for writers. They let you see how things actually look, and more importantly, how big they are relative to other things.

Museums are the perfect place to go if you want to learn how different objects can be perceived using different senses.

Take notes and snap photos of anything pertinent to your investigations.

Zoos

Most cities have at least one zoo of one sort or another. If you want to get an idea of how animals look, act, sound or smell, nothing beats visiting a zoo.

Botanical Gardens

Another great, and usually underused, resource is botanical gardens. It is likely that you can find a botanical garden within easy driving distance of where you live, especially if you're close to a major city.

In the Los Angeles area, the *Huntington Library* and the *Los Angeles County Arboretum and Botanic Garden* are both fantastic resources to learn about plant life. In a small area of a few hundred acres, each of these gardens reproduce several environments with thousands of species of plant life that you view, touch and smell.

Botanical gardens are great to visit if you want to understand plant life and get an idea of the sizes in relation to each other. How tall is a particular type of tree? How do thistles look in the field? Botanical gardens will give you the answers to these kinds of questions.

Reenactments

Virtually every city and town of any size hosts one or more reenactment groups. These might be known as Renaissance festivals, Civil War reenactments, Revolutionary war reenactments, and even World War II shows.

For example, the Renaissance fair in Irwindale, California, which is just outside of Los Angeles, is a great place to go to get an idea of how things smell, feel or taste in a pseudo-Renaissance period. It's theatrical rather than historical, but it gives you a feel for costumes, the spectacle of a joust, and what period weapons actually look like.

Civil War reenactments are also interesting and can help you understand how the weapons and other items of that time period worked, smelled, and looked.

National, State and Local Parks

Your tax dollars fund national, state, and local parks. These exist all over the United States, and in many other countries as well. There's usually a small fee for entrance, and they can be invaluable references to learn about the land and relative sizes.

If you live in the western United States, there are many dozens of national parks and hundreds of state parks where you can learn about desert life and scenery. You can also find ghost towns, both abandoned or in use as tourist attractions, to help your research.

Sketch

Create a sketch to get an idea of where things are in relation to each other, and to help determine what your point of view character can see.

This is for your own reference — no need for artistry. The goal is to understand what a character can see and perceive from their position in the space.

For example, if the scene is taking place in a room with the fireplace, quickly sketch the room and the location of the fireplace, the furniture, and anything else of significance. Visualize the characters in the sketch and use that to describe the scene from the character's point of view.

This can be a great way to keep track of where objects and characters are located as you write your story. I'll sometimes use a sketch with a few pieces from a monopoly game to represent characters and move them around as I write the story. This helps me keep everything straight and consistent.

Libraries

Don't forget the libraries in your local area. These are fantastic resources for finding books, magazines and other information that can be useful to build your understanding of your subject matter.

Many libraries host writing groups, critique circles, and author events — worth checking the board by the door.

Stock photos

Stock photo sites are an excellent place to find pictures of virtually anything that you can conceive of. You're not purchasing anything — just browsing for reference.

Some excellent stock photo sites include:

Depositphotos includes over 80 million photos and several million videos on virtually every conceivable subject. Pixabay offers images free of charge, with over a million photos available.

Google Image Search is also useful for a quick visual reference. You can't use these on your blog, in your book or anywhere else without violating copyright, but you can certainly look at them.

Maps

Google Maps and Bing Maps are great online tools to help you visualize the distance between places, the layout of streets and the distance between locations, as well as street-level views.

Let's say your story is about two spies working out of Berlin. Both Google Maps and Bing Maps can give you maps of the city.

Both services can also show the same area in satellite view.

You can also get street views, which are pictures of the surroundings of an address at street level. For example, if you wanted to see what a building looks like, you can zero in using Street view.

Both services also offer aerial views that let you survey a location from above.

When you're researching a location, mapping tools are invaluable.

Tours

Most businesses and public establishments offer tours to the general public. A factory tour is worth taking — I once toured the Jelly Belly factory in Northern California and the sensory details carried directly into a manuscript.

To find out if a tour is offered, jump on the website for the business or public establishment. Usually, they'll have it listed. If not, give them a call and ask.

Tours can be invaluable to help you understand how something looks from the inside. This is great for factories, mines, retail businesses, trucking companies, shipping companies, and so forth.

Movies and Television

Movies and television are generally not great places to get information that is realistic. The way the courts operate in *Law & Order* and the way forensics is done on *CSI* bears no resemblance to reality.

You can still use movies and television to get a feeling for what the subject is like. For example, if you want to learn how travel in space in our solar system might work, look at the SyFy channel's series *The Expanse*. This series has some pretty good representations of how a space battle might work, the effects of acceleration and gravity, and what it would mean to live on an asteroid.

Just remember: what you see in movies and television is a fictional representation, dramatized and compressed to fit the runtime.

Other Methods

Local police departments offer ride-alongs, which means you can sit in the back seat of a police car as they go about their day. You can experience the daily routine and see what police officers really do. The experience can add an element of reality to your crime drama or mystery story.

If you're writing a story that includes criminal or civil proceedings, sit in a courtroom. These are usually open to the public. All you need to do is show up, go inside, and sit down. Jury duty, if it comes your way, is another form of direct research.

Summing it up

In a world saturated with screens, people lose touch with direct experience. It's one thing to see a court case on *Law & Order*, and it's quite another to sit in a courtroom and learn what it is really like.

Looking at a picture of plants or animals on the Internet can give you some information that will be useful in your story. Visiting a botanical garden or a zoo to observe how plants and animals look, feel, smell and so on can help you write a much more vivid and entertaining story.

About the Author

Richard Lowe spent 33 years in the computer and information technology industry before ditching corporate life to pursue his real passion: writing and helping other writers succeed.

During his corporate days, he climbed the ranks to Vice President of Consulting and spent twenty years as Director of Computer Operations at Trader Joe's, focusing on computer security and disaster preparedness. When he finally escaped the cubicle world, he dove headfirst into professional ghostwriting.

Richard has ghostwritten books on everything from cybersecurity to artificial intelligence, retirement planning to office cleaning, and even a memoir for an Afghan politician. Companies like KnowBe4 have hired him to update major publications, and he's tackled topics ranging from the Internet of Things to Scrum methodologies.

When he's not writing, Richard photographs Renaissance festivals and belly dance events. He's documented over 1,200 dance performances and 400 festivals, plus spent years capturing the Tournament of Roses Parade. This attention to vivid detail shows up in his writing instruction too.

Richard's approach to writing advice comes from real-world experience in both corporate communication and creative storytelling. He's worked through the same challenges every writer faces, which makes his guidance practical instead of theoretical.

Learn more at thewritingking.com

Conclusions

Showing and telling are not opposites. They are tools. The best fiction uses both, deliberately, in balance — showing the moments that matter most, telling the moments that connect them. The skill is knowing which is which, and the only way to develop that skill is to read with attention and write with honesty.

The more you show — action, sensation, specific detail, characters in motion — the more readers are drawn into the world you're building. The more you tell, the more they observe it from a distance. Neither is wrong. Distance is sometimes what you need. But when a moment matters, be inside it.

What to Do Next

The techniques in this book work because they change the relationship between your reader and your story. Telling keeps the reader outside, observing. Showing pulls them in, experiencing. Every time you choose a concrete detail over an abstract label, a specific verb over a weak one with an adverb, a scene over a summary, you are choosing immersion over observation.

That choice becomes habit with practice. The first draft is where you discover the story. The revision is where you apply these techniques — where you find the places you've reported rather than shown, named rather than embodied, summarized what should be lived.

Start small. Take one scene from your current work and go through it with these questions: Where am I telling what I could show? Where am I naming emotions instead of letting behavior carry them? Where am I explaining what the reader could experience? The answers will point you toward better drafts.

The Self-Editing Checklist

Have I eliminated most emotion words like angry, sad, and happy? Did I replace weak verbs with strong, specific ones? Are my characters doing things rather than being things? Can the reader draw their own conclusions from the evidence I've provided? Have I used concrete, sensory details instead of abstract descriptions? Does each scene immerse the reader rather than report to them?

Technique and Voice

Everything in this book is a tool. Tools don't make things — writers make things. Two writers can apply every technique in this book and produce completely different results, because what sits on top of technique is voice: the particular temperature of a writer's prose, the rhythm they bring to a sentence, the specific things they notice and the specific way they render them.

Voice is not something you develop by studying it. It develops through practice, through writing a lot and reading carefully, through making choices and discovering which ones feel true to you. The techniques in this book remove the obstacles to voice — filter words, emotion labels, and explained images all muffle the writer's individual frequency. When you strip them out, what's left is more you.

This is why two writers who have both mastered showing produce such different prose. Alice Munro's showing is dense with interior time and retrospect. Elmore Leonard's is surface and dialogue and almost no interiority at all. Both are masterful. Both would score well on every checklist in this book. The difference is not technique — it is sensibility, which is another word for voice.

Use these techniques to clear the channel. Then trust what comes through it.

A Final Word

The hardest thing about showing is trusting the reader. Most telling comes from anxiety — the writer afraid that readers won't understand, won't feel it, won't get there on their own. So they explain. They label. They summarize.

Trust them. Readers are active participants. When you show them a woman blowing out a birthday candle she lit for herself, they understand the loneliness, the hurt, the waiting. You don't need to tell them. The moment carries everything if you let it.

Your job is to create the experience, not explain it. Write the scene. Then get out of the way.

Practice: The Revision Habit

Take a paragraph from your current work and circle every instance of: was, felt, seemed, looked, appeared. For each one, rewrite the sentence to show instead of tell. Most writers are surprised by how many there are — and how much stronger the passage becomes without them.

About the Author

Richard Lowe is a professional ghostwriter, writing instructor, and the author of the Short and Sweet Writing Guides series. He has ghostwritten over a hundred books across genres ranging from cybersecurity and artificial intelligence to memoir, business, and fiction — which means he has spent years studying exactly what separates manuscripts that work from manuscripts that don't.

He spent twenty years as Director of Computer Operations at Trader Joe's before leaving corporate life to write full time. The transition taught him something that shows up throughout his instruction: the habits that make writing clear in technical contexts — precision, specificity, showing rather than asserting — are the same habits that make fiction vivid.

Richard photographs Renaissance festivals, belly dance performances, and the Tournament of Roses Parade. More than 1,200 documented performances have given him a particular eye for the specific detail that captures a moment — the same eye this book tries to teach.

Show Don't Tell is part of the Working Writer's Library, a series designed to give writers the tools they can use immediately. No theory for its own sake. Just technique.

Learn more at **thewritingking.com**

Books By Richard Lowe

https://masterofworlds.com

Get free publishing insights and industry updates at *https://thewritingking.substack.com*

For ghostwriting and book coaching services see *https://thewritingking.com*

www.ingramcontent.com/pod-product-compliance
Lightning Source LLC
Chambersburg PA
CBHW031333060726
47590CB00007B/2448

9781946458551